The Ghost Excavation:

An Ethnography of a Haunted Site

John G. Sabol
C.A.S.P.E.R. Research Center

Also by John Sabol

Ghost Excavator (2007)

Ghost Culture (2007)

Gettysburg Unearthed (2007)

Battlefield Hauntscape (2008)

The Anthracite Coal Region (2008)

The Politics of Presence (2008)

Bodies of Substance, Fragments of Memory (2009)

Phantom Gettysburg (2009)

Digging Deep (2009)

The Re-Haunting(s) of Gettysburg (2010)

The Haunted Theatre (2011)

Ghost Culture Too (2012)

Beyond the Paranormal (2012)

Digging-Up Ghosts (2nd publishing, 2013)

Burnside Bridge (2013)

The Gettysburg Experience (2013)

The Absence Above, A Presence Below (2013)

The Production of Haunted Space (2013)

Centralia, Pennsylvania (2013)

The Ghost Excavation:

An Ethnography of a Haunted Site

Ghost Excavator Books, Inc™©

Bedford, Pennsylvania, USA

ISBN-13: 978-1494234676
ISBN-10: 149423467X

Ghost Excavation Books, Inc. ™©
A division of C.A.S.P.E.R. Research Center™©,
Bedford, PA, USA
www.ghostexcavation.com

"Social relations are performed not only around what is there, but sometimes also around the presence of what is not".

- *Kevin Hetherington, Sociologist (2004)*

Introduction

What is a haunting? Is it a series of "anomalous" objects/manifestations that can be measured and recorded; or is it an "event", a cultural performance, a habitual act that occurred in the life of a now "dead" human being? What gives "life" to a haunting? Is it a contemporary belief, a field "experience" during a "ghost hunt", an "entertaining" moment on "paranormal TV", the continuing presence of the past, or a phenomenon yet to be defined and identified?

The continued efforts by researchers, fieldworkers, and academics who live and work within the view that the way which science arbitrarily reduces the world into parts, separated one from another is correct, is largely responsible for us (as humans) to continue to not being able to communicate (consistently) with an afterlife consciousness that may survive the physical death of the body and brain!

A side-bar of this scientific reductionism has been the rise of a "paranormal"-based TV programming aimed at "entertaining" the public. This has furthered lengthened the gap between what is (now) public knowledge of "normality" and what is perceived to be "para-normal". Not only has this further alienated the scientific community that is largely responsible for this "para-division", it has led to a cottage industry in "hunting" ghosts (such as "ghost tourism"; "para-horror conventions"; "para-celebrity events/hunts", to name a few).

Ghosts (or "phantoms"; "spirits") are forms of life that can become present, I propose, when one understands how to represent what was their reality, both socio-cultural and semiotic. Research at a haunted location is a re-acclimatized sensory process of knowing how to represent oneself (and one's group of serious investigators) as active participants in their past, not contemporary, world view.

This is not a clinical view of past presence at a "haunted" location. It is an empathetic one! What we must do at these haunted locations is ethnographic work. This is not so much an ethnography of a particular culture in space, as it is a comparative analysis of various "ghost cultures" through time.

This is descriptive fieldwork. It is the use of a particular methodology (immersion into and participation in specific belief systems, anchored by that culture's "ritualistic" activities). It involves analysis and interpretations of meaning that <u>follow</u> rather than <u>precede</u> the ethnographic process in fieldwork:

"Ritual activities frequently involve a practical remembering effected through the experience and manifestation of symbolic material items (Barth 1987:35).

This enables field performance practices (those that are contextual to a specific space, time, and culture) to have meaning, and thus be recognized and recalled from memory.

This is directed fieldwork and a direction of analysis that comes from personal experiences in the field, and which leads to a theory about what "haunts" us at particular locations. The field practices of immersion and participation open new forms of cultural expressions. This re-directs or expands our behavior into other practices while still in the field.

Subsequently, what results from these manifestations is the development of hypotheses that serve us as the basis for subsequent research in the field, itself arising from the empiricism of the initial participatory practices. All of these participatory field acts are framed within particular social contexts and the engagement of past "actors" in these contexts, at a specific (and known) level of past production.

These past productions, the "subjects" of ethnographic fieldwork at haunted locations, create horizons of meaning that haunt the spaces at these locations. They form the "who", "what", and "why" of a continuing presence there. The personal perception of a manifesting presence at these locations is an experience-near acquisition of knowledge. The action of acquiring this knowledge is important because:

"knowledge is no longer conceived as something passive, but is more like an action; it affects things" (Baert 2005:163).

But we must "translate" (and transform) that experience-near knowledge into a methodology by which we can "control" (as much as possible) the "who", "what", and "why", of those manifestations, while investigating in the field at these historical and culturally-diverse haunted locations.

This methodology has evolved, personally for me, into what I conceive of as a "ghost excavation", based on my extensive experience in the field in "haunted" (and "ruined") locations, spanning more than four decades; and my academic training in anthropology, archaeology, history, sociology, and theatre.

A "ghost excavation" is first-person research, in which subjective knowing (immersing one's self into a particular culture's set of beliefs and ritualistic behaviors) is central to the fieldwork. Since this immersion, as participation, is potentially compromising, the "ghost excavation" is enacted within a specific set of controls that follow a commonality of procedures (see below).

The (ethnographic) process is meant to be dynamic (as participant), as opposed to a general reliance on observation and the recording of data through scientific measuring devices (specifically "ghost gear": EMF meters; casual EVP through audio recorders; thermal scans; K-2 meters and the like; "ghost box" recordings, etc.).

The "ghost excavation" is a research method that is concerned with re-conceptualizing fieldwork (and distancing itself from a "ghost hunt"), and concerns itself with those vague, ephemeral, and (the possibility of) multiple cultural realities that may be embedded at a haunted location.

It is similar to the work of sociologist John Law (e.g. 2004), who argues that research methods in the social sciences are performative in nature, constituting a particular way of framing the object of research (2004:141-54). This is an emphasis on process over product (doing rather than collecting). It is a research strategy that accepts a degree of indefiniteness, and certainly aids to undermine the fragmentation of realities into binary opposites (such as natural/supernatural; active/passive; and us/"other") so common today in scientific "reality".

This is the world of a "ghost excavation", and here is how this methodology can work and be used at a haunted location.....

Table of Contents

Introduction......................... 6

Table of Contents................... 12

Photographs........................ 15

The Politics of Contemporary
Presence............................. 17

An Archaeology of (for) the
Future................................. 28

Legacy................................. 31

The Components of a "Ghost
Excavation" Methodology........... 35

Important Component in "Ghost
Excavation".......................... 39

Landscape........................... 39

Sensitivity and Common Sense. 43

Addendum....................... 52

Time and Ritual................... 58

Performance...................... 64

The Poetics...................... 74

The Craft........................ 82

The Prequel...................... 86

Archaeology (Metaphor and Field Practice).............................. 91

Place Attachment................. 103

The "Ghost Culture"............. 120

Horizon of Meaning.............. 124

Representation and Communication...................... 129

Memory........................... 133

Experiential Fieldwork.......... 143

"P.O.P." (Participate-Observe-Perform)........................... 148

The "Ghost Script" and Haunting Storyboards"........................ 154

Summary........................... 161

Appendixes........................ 172

The Haunted Sensorium......... 172

The Haunting "Gesture": The Codification of Interactive Presence.............. 175

On the "Scent" of a "Cultural Gesture"............................ 187

Haunted Aural Awareness....... 192

Haunted Spatial Awareness..... 198

Haunted Nodal Spatial System. 207

The Mapping of Haunted Space. 212

Bibliography.......................... 217

Biographical Note................... 227

Photographs

1. "Ghost Excavations" in the Field.. 34
2. My "Ghosts of Place"............... 43
3. Working at Cholula in 1970........ 47
4. Working at Cholula in 1970........ 48
5. A "Ghost Excavation"............... 49
6. The Palenque Rubbing (1966).... 53
7. Temple of the Inscriptions (Palenque, Mexico 1970)....................... 56
8. Temple of the Inscriptions (Today)............................... 57
9. A Performance "Ritual" in the Field.................................... 63
10. The Cultural Scenario as a "Tool" of Research............................ 73
11. "Ghost Excavations" in the Field.................................... 81
12. Introducing the Field of Inquiry: Preliminary Discussions............. 86
13. Fieldwork Operations at Burnside Bridge, Antietam Battlefield (Maryland)........................... 96

14. Fieldwork at a Haunted Location............................ 99

15. Exploring Ft. Mississauga (Ontario, Canada) (1813-1855)............... 102

16. The "Jogger" at Burnside Bridge.................................. 104

17. Cultural Scenario Enacted at Burnside Bridge (2010)......................... 117

18. Cultural Scenario Enacted at Burnside Bridge (2011)......................... 118

19. Cultural Scenario Enacted at Burnside Bridge (2012)....................... 119

20. Establishing "Identity"......... 132

21. What Memories Still Remain of this Performance Practice of Space?.. 138

22. Using the "P.O.P." Method in Fieldwork............................. 152

23. Another Example of Using "P.O.P."................................. 153

24. Alvin Flint........................... 170

25. The "Empty" Grave Site of William Holmes................................ 171

26. The Author....................... 226

<u>The Politics of</u>
<u>Contemporary Presence</u>

In the words of that great archaeologist and Egyptologist Flinders Petrie:

"I here live and do not scramble to fit myself to the requirements of others".

"It is the living that chase away the 'ghosts', and not the 'ghosts' that make the living run from reality".

- **The "Ghost Excavation" philosophy**

As a trained anthropologist, I am always between one cultural horizon and another, somewhere in time. I was enculturated into the Western way of being, but I have frequently journeyed to become immersed into the "other" cultures of non-Western societies. I live in the United States, but I have journeyed and worked frequently outside those geographical boundaries. I am situated in one space, but there are times (too many) that I think of other spaces.

Anthropology is a science where observation, participation, description, and purpose are "entertained", but are not forms of entertainment. The purpose of fieldwork in anthropology (the ethnography) is to describe the conditions and potentiality of human life.

This human life, as revealed in ethnographic fieldwork, does not begin and end, in many cultures, in a specific time or particular space. It keeps on manifesting, with situation and purpose in mind. Individual experience is the producer of this process, which creates history and cultural traditions. This experience is humanly possible, and the history is uniquely human. It is this unique human ethnographic history that we will explore here.

Also, as a trained archaeologist, I "dig" through multiple temporalities at sites, and "unearth" (or "recover") concepts and expressions of culture that alter that present situated moment in space and work in the field. During the excavation process, I am embedded in multiple liminal positions, a perfect location for researching and "digging" through a haunting. It begets a philosophy that warrants a number of apprehensions about how to define our contemporary reality.

As an archaeologist, I have, for the past several decades now, chosen to carry out <u>my</u> "excavations" (for the most part without institutional funding or academic affiliations) in what Loren Eiseley has called the **"Night Country" (cf. Eiseley 1972).** These "excavations" are not for all archaeologists. They are a choice. As Eiseley writes:

"If you cannot bear the silence and the darkness, do not go there.... (1972:15).

This darkness, and it attendant sensory expressions, hide knowledge and presences that are, for the most part, lost and forgotten today. These are places, and spaces within places, where time folds, enfolds, unfolds, and expands reality, not encasing that reality in a secure box and calling it something "paranormal". These are the spaces I "excavate", and in the darkness of those spatial enclosures, there remain presences that wait to be "recovered" and heard (again).

A "ghost" (or "apparition") co-occupies a similar position and situation: between two worlds, and various spaces and temporalities. A haunted site is a location of ambiguity, someplace in time and perception between absence and presence, silence and "soundings", and that moment when something becomes an unexpected reality. The liminal, once confined to the anthropological literature, has become a <u>normal</u> sense that illuminates the experiential multiplicities of human life at haunted locations, for both the "life" of the "ghost" and for the "lifework" of this investigator.

"Ghosts" and contemporary people in these liminal positions are actors that must find paths to walk toward or walk away from. There are individual solutions that must be met, both in space (walk within a different space) and in time ("dig down" or remain bound). The steps that are taken become a "badge" of identity. In this liminal position, the researcher is no longer an objective <u>observer</u> that merely records and measures. Instead, participation becomes a requirement of the fieldwork. The "ghost" loses its image of superficiality as an "actor" in an empty theatre, and becomes present and known in a contemporary setting.

Fieldwork is action, and a re-action to acts, a flow away from "center-stage", the "ego" dimension, to one going beyond the edge of what is currently known. Archaeologists in the field occupy a unique position in this liminal situation. We know that something can be there prior to excavation, but can only become present through the field performance practices of an excavation.

Thus, the excavation, betwixt and between a potential manifestation, allows the archaeologist to become a witness through the participatory process, a process that parallels fieldwork as a "ghosting" of similar fieldwork in the past. But it becomes a "ghost excavation" in haunted, liminal, space.

The key to exit this liminality, this uncertainty of presence, is the performed act that recovers <u>pre-existing</u> remains of past presence. Presence, during the excavation process, leaves the liminality of a "ghostly" presence, and becomes human again. The "ghost" no longer remains an "anomaly", as something betwixt and between some object of manifestation that lies <u>beyond</u> understanding and meaning.

What I am about to say now may be politically incorrect, but the nature of "paranormal politics" dictates that it be said. If it offends anyone who reads this, then maybe you should pause for a moment, take a deep breath, and look very critically at what you are doing in the field at haunted locations!

Contemporary "ghost hunting", like its "haunted" history going back to the days of Elliot O'Donnell in the late 19th c., works within a restricted territory of presence; most of the time, this is <u>not</u> a haunted space. The "hunting" of ghosts is a popular cultural trope, inspired today, unfortunately, by the unreality of paranormal TV programming, itself fueled by unimaginative producers.

The producers of these shows should follow what Lynn Poole, writer, producer, and star of various science-related TV series said back in 1952:

"Play it honestly and factually and give the viewer credit for intelligence".

Poole's comment comes back to "haunt" us in this time of reality TV. These productions are not only uniquely unscientific; they have become quite boring (and repetitive) entertainment pieces. They have created unwittingly, a "monster". It is that "monstrosity" that has largely determined what most "paranormal" investigators experience in the field, and how they interpret what they experience. Back in the 1950's, Poole wanted to see real experts, not imitators, or actors (something all too common in reality TV today)!

Given this popular (and highly lucrative) format as entertainment, "ghost hunting" has frozen the view of the reality that can confront the investigation of haunted space. Instead of "opening" the field for relevant and meaningful (even progressive) exploration, "ghost hunting" has erased any potential insights through the closure of public attitude toward this type of "research".

"Ghost hunting", as a popular contemporary cultural trope, involves a particular politics of presence. This "politics" narrows the investigative field of inquiry by "ghosting" what others say and do (based both on this TV programming and what people say and "exhibit" on social networks). This "exhibitionism" also limits what <u>cannot</u> be said and done, lest one offends a large sector of the "ghost hunting" community!

A typical, popular version of the "ghost hunt" inhibits what can be made present, what is kept absent, and what remains largely "invisible" as solid investigative fieldwork. The TV shows and the "para-celebrity" events have the power that controls the processes in the field. It has become a critical issue for serious investigators.

"Ghost hunting", unfortunately, has left a biased footprint upon ghost research: potential objective analysis turned around to subjective entertainment and/or egocentric attempts at those "15 minutes of fame". Most of these endeavors have reduced the legitimacy of this type of research, and it has become all too often rightfully criticized by academic disciplines that do so in the name of one science or another; or, one skeptic after another.

Ghost research, besides its <u>social</u> science baseline, must also become a moral science-based discipline. It must begin to explore the ways in which interactive cultural presence (both past <u>and</u> present) must regulate their associations with one another. Fieldwork at haunted locations is, at times, immediately and directly implicated in the past world that remains. This immerses the investigator into certain behavioral implications: how s/he conducts themselves in the field. A "demand and command" attitude and stance is morally unacceptable, even (especially) as entertainment. This reflects the attitude we have toward ourselves!

Doing fieldwork at haunted locations assumes great moral responsibility in our "signs" and representations toward these (possible) presences. If we dismiss understanding <u>their</u> world, we devalue their presence, the result of which turns a past cultural expression (as an <u>intentional</u> "sign" of communication) into an "anomaly" and "paranormal" event......

Let us begin anew.....with a <u>different</u> perspective:

"So now then we begin again this history of us"

- **Gertrude Stein, 1925.**

"To go forward, one has to go back.

To go back, one has to turn around.

To turn around, one has to pull over and look to

See if anyone was coming".

- **Linda Mussman,** *Civil War Chronicles* (1988)

Are you coming...on this road to the "ruin"?

"For I know some will say, why does he make us hobble after him over broken stones, decayed buildings, and old rubbish"?

- **George Wheeler,** *A Journey Into Greece (1682)*

When we excavate ruins, be they haunted or not, we unearth our own future, not the past. We should heed well this meaning, the memory of decay, and learn from it. What remains after the past can indicate the nature of an unfolding (continuing) drama, a percolating contemporary past, and our presence within.

A "dig" exposes that moment in time when we find, while still living, those moments that can "haunt" our future......

An Archaeology of the Future

Let us, in the words of anthropologist Marilyn Strathern, "create the conditions for new thoughts" (1988:20).

Once upon a time, archaeologists unearthed the past through excavations into the earth. Today, archaeological field performances can open a space on the surface, permitting traces of the past to be recovered. These traces are more than the residual elements of the "ghosts of place". They are an exploration into the continued "afterlife", not of structures, burials, or artifact assemblages, but of forms of (human) cultural life.

These "excavations" reveal more than a re-constructed time travel, such as "living histories", re-enactments, computer gaming, and the elaboration of virtual worlds. These are remains that are live, alive, and real.

It is the notion of a recognizable reality that those, once thought dead and buried, are still active actors of past cultural ways, who continue to perform today as if it were yesterday. It is archaeological work with "who" remains of these forms of life, at locations popularly perceived as "haunted".

This archaeology of the past as future addresses:

- What it means to <u>still</u> be human;
- "Who" are these "ghosts", as members of particular past human groups; and
- How alternative forms of life are cultural expressions, or "signs", of continuing presence.

These remains go beyond mere cultural heritage. They become a social recognition for these forms of life. It moves "who" remains from a description of past presence to an alternative way of past life presence in the present-future.

"This happened here...."What" and "Who" remains? We can get a picture of the past from both what we can see on the surface, and what we can recover still from the surface of multiple manifesting pasts.

But there is more: a sense of the past that goes beyond material remains and presence observed and recorded in "traditional" archaeological excavation. There becomes a sensing of the past, as it is encountered through immersive acts and performance practices in the field. This is a "ghost excavation", and this is a book on what those excavations can mean to all of us today.

<u>Legacy</u>

"The way we are living
Timorous or bold,
Will have been our life".

- **Seamus Heaney, "Elegy"**

This is about a life in the field. These are no ordinary fields, cultivated and growing. It is, rather, about work in spaces that are perceived as "haunted" by a continuation of past presence. What follows are storyboards, not completed scripts. I do not make this decision. It is their "call", those that remain.....

As I write, words plow into one another, creating openings. This "open ground" is a place of excavation. It is about a real life, not one invented for entertainment. It is a life that breathes with the past. Though the ground is deeply mined, cultural remains continue to surface. These remains make sense, as the ghosts emerge and are revealed.

In these pages, between the words, one will encounter a "ghost excavation". What becomes unearthed are some buried ideas, remains that become fragments of past memories of experiences. This "ghost excavation", in the fields haunted by past presences, becomes a visitation by a past that is present still. It is a landscape of ruin, but one which still remains occupied in visual absence....by "ghosts"!

To enter these fields, we must leave the present for the moment and focus on the world of "what" and "who" remains in these fields. This involves extensive archaeological "excavation" and intensive ethnographic "immersion". The fieldwork recovers an entropic space where memory has halted time, though activity and purpose remain active.

These memories, past but remaining present, speak loudly of discontinuous times, acts, and events. These are layered memories, a palimpsest of biographical pages, some erased, while others are quite ephemeral. Though there are remains, so much is lost that,

"what do we say anymore

To conjure the salt of our earth?

So much comes and is gone

That should be crystal and kept".

- **Seamus Heaney, "The Singer's House"**

When we enact a ghost excavation in the field, we transform the memory. We, however, must allow this transformation to resonate – to be poetic, not chaotic, to those who continue to remain behind. This is the <u>least</u> that we can do for them. This is how we begin our work in these haunted fields......

Photo 1: Ghost Excavations in the Field

John Sabol with James Castle at the ruins of a caretaker's cottage...

The Components of a Ghost Excavation Methodology

Anthropologist Tim Ingold, in an editorial for *Man* (1992), argues that life involves the passage of time in which an anthropological framework is inadequate to define. We need an archaeological sensibility to those "ethno-stratas" of cultural behavior and expression that continue to surface and manifest at haunted sites. Ghost research, as the study of past ethnographic cultures and their "surviving" participants, must adopt an archaeological sensitivity in order to deal with "what" (past cultural expressions) and "who" (past "actors" as surviving "ghosts") remains from the past, perhaps multiple cultural pasts.

The concepts of enfolding time, and an unfolding presence, as the <u>interactive</u> "ghosts of place", are potentially unifying concepts in ghost research that an archaeological approach (as a form of "excavation") is capable of recovering. Past acts of behavior and ritual performances can come into being through contemporary contextual (and resonating) space-specific investigative performances.

If we don't attempt to <u>extend</u> our concept and categories of "forms of life", then we conceal (rather than recover) the "life" of "others". We reduce their manifestations to mere "anomalies" or "paranormal" events. The bottom line, after "digging even deeper" is this: we can't explain what we don't accept as possible or something beyond our present frame of <u>restricted</u> reality!

What follows are some basic concepts that allow us to take that first step, however small it may be, toward that expansion and transformation of ghost research.

"Man is an animal suspended in webs of significance that he himself has spun. I take culture to be those webs, and the analysis of it not an experimental science in search of

laws, but an interpretive one, in search of meaning".

- **Clifford Geertz, anthropologist (1973:5)**

In an unpublished beginning of his autobiography, Loren Eiseley, archaeologist and poet (and one of my favorite authors) has written:

"Though I am an archaeologist by profession, there are tombs for my life I would not enter, vaults through whose doorways, I would not descend....There is a shadow on the wall before me. It is my own. I write in a borrowed room at midnight. Tomorrow the shadow on the wall will be that of another. Very well, huntsman, let the hunt begin" (June 20, 1963: quoted in *Fox at the Wood's Edge: A Biography of Loren Eiseley* **by Gale E. Christianson, 1990).**

For me, Eiseley's "hunt" is my "ghost excavation", and in that "ghost excavation", I do journey into "haunted" landscapes. I do enter past "tombs" of cultural memories; and I do cross doorways that lead me into other realities, <u>all</u> of which are <u>still</u> human in nature!

Loren Eiseley was very interested in the paranormal. There is no question about that. He purchased many books on the subject, including one written by archaeologist T.C. Lethbridge, *Ghost and Ghoul* (1962), a thorough analysis of residual hauntings. He and his wife, Mabel, also experimented with the Ouija board, and Mabel **"began receiving spirit messages….a year or two later" (Christianson 1990:72).**

This book on "ghost excavations" is dedicated to the memory of Loren Eiseley who inspired me to "think outside the box" by looking at the world and reality from a different perspective….

Important Components in a "Ghost Excavation" Landscape

"The archaeology of the landscape constitutes a line of research whose objective is to study archaeological remains in accordance with the spatial coordinates in which human action has taken place" **(Mendez 1998:57).**

Loren Eiseley, poet, nature writer, and archaeologist once said:

"Some landscapes....refuse history. Some efface it so completely, it is never found. In others, the thronging of memories of the past subdue the present".

It is within these landscapes, as a landscape <u>as</u> memory, that haunts us today with their presence.

Certain landscapes, however, produce particular remains, some of which basic excavation methodologies do not readily recover. Archaeologist Jacquetta Hawkes, in her *Guide to the Prehistoric and Roman Monuments of England and Wales* (1951) has said this:

"....perhaps places where men had felt intensely and acted violently never quite rid themselves of the effects; perhaps such feelings are created only in the minds of later beholders- yet even so, their survival is real".

One such landscape was an American Civil War battlefield. On a Civil War battlefield, human actions (both pre-battle and intense combat) occurred within a particular landscape defined militarily as the "K.O.C.O.A.". It is within these "K.O.C.O.A." spaces, I propose, that some effects (and continuing presence) of battlefield "active" remains survive today.

This present work attempts to unearth the power of memory in particular landscapes, such as these Civil War battlefields. It focuses on how "ghostly" manifestations, as fragments of remembered experiences, can become meaningful today, <u>and</u> have long-lasting consequences. Memory, I believe, is at its most powerful, and it's most fragile, in the hands of one who is an archaeologist, as one who "digs" deeply into the past to bring other "worlds" and individuals back to life in the present.

The excavation, as the memory process itself, is based on certain decisions (sometimes independently "surfacing") about what Rudyard Kipling has called his **"six honest serving men"**. These are those who taught him all his knowledge. Their names were: "How", "Where", "When", "Why", "What" and "Who". These are the six "ghosts" that we attempt to unearth in a field methodology called a "ghost excavation".

This archaeological practice of a "ghost excavation" eliminates, I propose, the arbitrary distinction that is made between a completed past and the continuing presence of that reality today. The goal of a "ghost excavation", through memory re-collection, is to effectively erase the once clear distinction (and difference) between "Life" and "Death".

Digging-deep into past memory patterns is more than an archaeological metaphor:

"Genuine memory must....yield an image of the person who remembers, in the same way a good archaeological report not only informs us about the strata from which its findings originate, but also gives an account of the strata which first had to be broken through" (Walter Benjamin, *Selected Writings,* *1999).*

This first stratum that must be broken through is the contemporary one in this landscape, and the associated tasks and beliefs that binds one to the present. The goal is to "dig" deep enough in order to "unearth" that which occupies the surface of today's past manifestations. In this ruined landscape, substance takes the form of presence. They rise and take hold, as the "excavation" begins......

<u>Sensitivity and Common Sense</u>

"Ghosts of the living and dead alike, of both individual and collective spirits, of both other selves and our own selves, haunt the places of our lives".

- **Michael Mayerfeld Bell, Environmental Sociologist**

Photo 2: My "Ghosts of Place"

The library of research and writing

T.C. Lethbridge, British archaeologist and paranormal investigator, once said that a ghost is **"something out of its normal earthly time sequence".** In that sense, that of temporality, <u>all</u> material remains unearthed during an archaeological excavation are "ghostly" remains. So too are the memories that we recover when remembering a past activity, a place, or an event. We are all haunted by these "ghosts". But, it is the archaeologist that encounters them on a daily basis in the field.

The writer, with an archaeological sensitivity to what remains from the past, also allows these ghosts to manifest through the words that resonate to a past experience. Loren Eiseley, as both archaeologist and writer, says it best:

"One exists in a universe convincingly real, where the lines are sharply drawn in black and white. It is only later, if at all, that one realizes the lines were never there in the first place....One must then simply deny the episode or adjust one's vision" (1975:100).

As that archaeologist and writer, I have preferred the latter in my fieldwork. The result is what I call a "ghost excavation".

I have also learned that there is a huge difference between being 10 years old and attaining one's 20th, and being 20 and celebrating a 60th birthday. It is a difference that is greater than the age difference. At 10, back in the early 1960's, I was a "ghost hunter", looking for a phantom experience (mostly in books). At 20, I began to excavate what I had read at 10, during archaeological work in many different "haunted fields". At 50, I began to remember and started to write about the experiences. During my 6th decade in this life, the work continues in earnest.

At this "stage" of my life, the excavation is still rift with holes, though the exploration continues for those lost traces. My writing tries to fill-in these holes and those experiences along the journey, despite the missing pieces. One must, however, be ever cautious. Excavations do not all produce material remains.

Sometimes, expectations are not met (and that is a good thing). Lethbridge states the obvious:

"One learns to recognize the great gulf which exists between those who really use their brains to solve important questions and those who think that anything can be answered if you dig a big enough hole".

I make no pretensions concerning my research, fieldwork, or writing. I can only say that I begin each excavation with a distinct purpose, and follow it through! I learned that, at 60, it was <u>not</u> time to slow-down. There was no concern for a mirrored image. Reflection was not a gaze, or a pause.

It was time, at middle age, to begin a new road, not head home to a relaxing engagement with the sofa and a favorite TV show! As the Roman poet Horace advised: **"start in the middle of things".** So I took his advice and continued in earnest with these "ghost excavations", betwixt and between archaeology and paranormal research.

During a break from my first archaeological excavation in Mexico (at Cholula in 1970), I was already traveling with the present dead. I had a copy of John L. Stephens's book about his journey through Guatemala and Mexico in the 1840's. When I had the opportunity, I made the trek to Palenque, as he did so many years before. I went alone, and the experience provided a wealth of experiences into places where the only inhabitants were the jungle fauna and flora. This trip, and those experiences, saw the actual birth of the "ghost excavation" methodology.

Photo 3: Working at Cholula in 1970

John Sabol on right

Photo 4: Working at Cholula in 1970

John Sabol on right

Since then, I have continued to excavate deep into the earth for traces of past humanity. The only difference is that today these "excavations" are surface probes of what still remains (on that surface) after the event have past. The two archaeological practices (deep/surface excavation) are similar, though.

Both require an immersed sensitivity to the past. They both attempt to unearth the memories of past cultural practices and/or past productions of space. Most importantly, both require an archaeological sensitivity, sensibility, and **"archaeological**

imagination" (Shanks 2012) to past presence and material remains.

Photo 5: A "Ghost Excavation"

Investigators Mike Stevenson (left) and James McCann (right)

I work within the gravesites of "ghosts". These are not necessarily the sites of the dead. These ghosts linger because they still project memories into the mirror. In contrast, the memory of the "true" dead is gone. It is the archaeologist who unearths this dead memory, most of the time in the field. But it is during a "ghost excavation" that an interactive memory from the past may still be unearthed.

Most archaeologists leave little direct impact on the culture(s) whose ruins they excavate. After all, most of the time their cultural subjects are long dead and buried. A "ghost excavation", however, lying outside the strict bounds of academia, can affect those who may remain. This is an important consideration for fieldwork.

The "ghost excavator" is a role that serves as a rite of passage between the present and the past. Fieldwork is not a transition between presence and absence. It is a performance between past stages, one becoming "actively" present and another long gone, but present in remains.

As an archaeologist and "ghost excavator", I have unearthed both sets of presences: those of the dead, and those of the still "living" dead. I have walked among both of these remains within the ruins of the past. In this fieldwork, time is not a continuum from this to that, here to there, or before to actual.

I don't just unearth the past. I make the future become a reality of the past, by allowing it to be a possibility beyond the present moment. A "ghost excavation" unfolds time: past, present, and future are one, contained in the same symmetrical space. It is a concept well-known to writers:

"I will visit a place

entirely other than myself.

Whether it is the future

or the past need not be

decided in advance".

- **Susan Sontag**

Addendum

Perhaps those early (in my "ghost excavation" career) journeys to Palenque (1970-72) were "historic" after all? They did resonate (in some small way) with Stephens's trek there in the 1840's. I <u>did</u> have some experiences then that today's visitor cannot have, and these experiences do reflect some aspects of that exploration of the ruins in the 1840's. For example, the contemporary park regulations at the Palenque National Park include the following (2008):

- **"Walk within the designated paths only".**
- **"Do not make any new trails to climb up and keep strictly on the trodden pathways and the main stairways..."**
- **"Do not turn over any stones".**
- **"By no means are visitors allowed to be within the ruins after hours".**
- **"No more permits are issued to visit Pacal's tomb".**
- **"Do not make any rubbings of the sculptures of Palenque".**

I did experience <u>all</u> of the above "restrictions" back in 1970, when I wandered through the ruins, unguided and unattended. Though I did not personally make any "rubbings", I do have in my possession (a gift from a friend) a "rubbing" that was made at Palenque in 1966.

Photo 6: The Palenque Rubbing (1966)

It was in 1962 that Merle Greene Robertson brought a new tool to Mayan studies. These were life-size rubbings she made at the ruins of Tikal in Guatemala. Since that time, she has made more than 2,000 rubbings. Her rubbings have revealed details of Mayan Society that have previously escaped the most experienced observers of Mayan ornamental sculpture.

Her contributions to Mesoamerican archaeology are invaluable. In 1994, she was awarded the "Order of the Aztec Eagle" by the Mexican Government, that nation's highest award to a non-national. Though my Palenque rubbing was not done by Robertson, it still is magnificent and is an early rubbing (and activity) that people cannot do any more at the ruins.

I know now that my various journeys to Palenque were much more than tourist excursions. They involved adventurous experiences and the uncovering of material remains (out there in the jungle beyond the ruins) that echoed, albeit to a much lesser degree, those experienced by John L. Stephens in the Palenque landscape of the 1840's. My memory is firmly attached to an archaeological legacy that cannot be duplicated by contemporary visits to the Palenque ruins.

Today, through the work of Robertson and others, the world of Palenque and the ancient Maya, and our knowledge of it, has greatly expanded, and new data is continuously being recovered. In an article, written in 1966 the year my rubbing was made at Palenque, Merle Greene Robertson wrote:

"Perhaps the most exciting rubbing that I ever did, and also the hardest....was the sarcophagus in the Temple of the Inscriptions at Palenque" (*Classic Maya Rubbings, page 34*).

Today, you cannot visit Pacal's Tomb in the Temple of the Inscriptions without special permission from the Park Director. That permission is granted for strictly scientific purposes. I retain both a memory of that tomb, deep inside the pyramid (and visited alone in 1970), and a rubbing from 1966, the year of Merle Robertson's rubbing in that same tomb.

The memory and that "artifact" are my "living" (and "haunting") remembrances that link a book read as a youth, the work of a contemporary archaeologist, and the personal experience of a (then) student of archaeology. Those resonating connections are but one basis for the birth of the "ghost excavation" methodology that I now practice in the field. Is it any wonder that the symbol (a Mayan glyph) for our research center is "C.A.S.P.E.R.", which represents the 2nd ruler (name unknown) of the Mayan city of Palenque, Mexico?

Photo 7: Temple of the Inscriptions (Palenque, Mexico, 1970)

Photo 8: Temple of the Inscriptions (Today)

Time and Ritual

Recently, ethnographers have become interested in incorporating history into their fieldwork narratives. Believing that an archaeological sensitivity and sensibility can help to better understand this historicism in investigating past cultures at haunted locations, I have developed a methodology called "ghost excavations".

This is a method in which to understand the present in a different way, as it relates to past presence. This is because we are working with what is left of that past in the present (Shanks 2012) as "this happened here" = "what remains?" It is a method that is based on the material remains of subjects as actors, in past performance practices enacted in the present that occur on the surface, and not objects that are recovered beneath the earth.

These traces and fragments of past human behaviors must be understood, I propose, as residuals of memory fields, as an emotional remnant from the past that "haunts" the living in the present. The use of an archaeological approach (to analyze a past ethnographic setting) may be what Walter Benjamin (1994:505) has called the detritus or rags of history. Loren Eiseley quite bluntly has said: **"Archaeology is the ghost of history" (Heuer 1987:242).**

Time and the materiality of what remains help define archaeology. In a "ghost excavation", there is a different concept of time with regards to "what" (and "who") may remain. At haunted locations, temporalities that define a form of life that <u>becomes</u> present, not one past and dead, can manifest as materialized memories that abolish the linearity of time.

Michael Flaherty, a sociologist, has introduced the concept of **"timework".** This is the production of particular experiences. A "haunting", I propose, is one example of this. Ritual acts are another.

This concept of ritual is important in a "ghost excavation". It's all about time. Bell (1997) defines ritual in this way:

"to do something in such a way that the doing itself gives the act a special....status" (1997:168).

Jack Hunter, in *The Anthropology of the Weird* in *Darklore* (Volume 6:243-253) has said:

"These types of experiences can be had by anyone so long as they participate in the relevant cultures and ritual situations....It requires our participation in the moment....in order to be experienced" (page 252).

The "attitude" in ritual performance, rather than the act itself, is critical. In a "ghost excavation", the "ritual" (in the form of contextual/resonating cultural scenarios: see below) is an experiment of what meaning was, and how it was practiced (socially-shared) in particular past cultures where some members may still "haunt" particular spaces.

This concept of "ritual" is particularly relative to "timework". It involves performance, not passive observation (or measurement). It involves a specific "attitude" in those performed "rituals": "as if one was" a participant in that past culture.

"Timework", through the "ritual" process in a "ghost excavation" (the enactment of performance scenarios relative to particular past cultural systems of belief) is a social technology of time manipulation, what archaeologist Julian Thomas has called a **"technology of memory" (1993).** This process of performance is not a measurement of time intervals. It is a <u>creation</u> of <u>social</u> intervals that folds into each other.

This means that the present is <u>not</u> uniquely present because past time has also endured, and is now being repeated. This "repeatability" ("unfolding" time) is achieved through social interaction (the cultural scenario in a "ghost excavation"). It creates "ritualistic" acts (as a "special status") in the present.

The "ritual" of performance practices in a "ghost excavation" unfolds time. This is because it enfolds entities (past and present) into a particular social situation, in a specific space, that <u>creates</u> (not deters) relationships and (intentional) communications. It is the contemporary performance (as ritualistic "timework") in a "ghost excavation", I propose, that manifests an interactive haunting at a particular "time" in specific spaces at a location. And these manifestations are <u>repeatable</u> when the "ritual" (as those contextual/resonating cultural scenarios) is re-performed at a later date.

In a "ghost excavation", we are interested in vertical, "deeply-dug" elements of past cultural knowledge: what remains of past occupations, rather than a horizontal measurement of contemporary space. This is a path clearly taken by Loren Eiseley in such writings as *The Night Country* (1972), a book that still inspires me and how and what I write about.

These "deeply-dug" penetrations into past memory fields through "ritualistic" performance acts, are always grounded in unstable terrain: haunted space. These are places subject to transformations without evolutionary (or temporal) tendencies.

These haunted spaces don't evolve, so much as they involve an unfolding trajectory (a "timelessness") of manifesting presences, expressing one past act after another (when the proper resonating "ritual" is enacted).

The concept of the cultural scenario, as a field performed "ritualistic" practice, embeds us within a ritual setting, permitting us to experience a particular past presence and cultural situation in the present. It is to this performance, as "ritual", that I will now "entertain" you.

Photo 9: A Performance "Ritual" in the Field

From left to right, John Sabol with Investigators Shian Gordan, James Castle, James McCann

<u>Performance</u>

"A thing which cannot be understood inevitably re-appears like an unlaid ghost".

- **Sigmund Freud**

A "ghost" or "spirit" is not always a passive, frozen in time (residual), entity that is "waiting" out there to be discovered. In a "ghost excavation", we focus on the "ghost" as a cultural being, who remembers (and realizes) particular aspects of their cultural "upbringing" through a fluid (and manifesting) process of creating meaning.

We propose that interaction with this cultural "form of life" is through performance practices that resonate with the memory of past meaningful behaviors that were once enacted in life by the entity. Fieldwork in a "ghost excavation" is an immersion into particular past cultural practices as a pedagogical device (Turner 1998:139-155).

This is not a form of **"practioner ethnography" (Bryman 2001).** An example of this "practioner" approach would be a psychic or medium who, as a practioner of psychic abilities, would use contextual performances to connect with particular past entities.

I agree with ethnographic film writers Barbash and Taylor who consider it important to regard **"life as it is lived rather than as it is reported on" (1997:36).** In a "ghost excavation", we do not rely on prior experiences of past occupants of a place, or of contemporary "ghost hunting" accounts of their experiences, measurements, and recordings.

We base a "ghost excavation" in performance practices that are contextual (and resonate with) a specific cultural (or ethnic) group, within a particular historical layer. This is based on "this happened here....what remains?" rather than "this happens here". A "ghost excavation", and the use of immersive cultural performances, occupies a liminal position betwixt/between ethno-archaeological work and "paranormal" research.

Through these performance practices, we "dig" for manifestations of interactive past presence as a "verb" ("becoming present"), not a "ghost" or "apparitional experience" as a noun (its presence or absence). "Show us a sign of your presence" does have meaning <u>when</u> there is a manifestation in context (and relative to these immersive performances), and not when one uses a direct "command and demand":

- This is them "showing us" (from the past), and not a command/demand of "show us" (from the present).

A "ghost excavation" is a form of performance ethnography, or an anthropology of experience (Turner 1992), as we also focus on important <u>past</u> rituals and performance events. An example of this would be the Inherent Military Probability behaviors of the Civil War soldier (part of the "ritual" of the "culture of war") that was learned in extensive drills, and performed on the battlefield.

In the field, we must always remember to dot the "I's":

- <u>Intervention</u>- Fieldwork becomes a <u>surface</u> "excavation" of "what" and "who" remains

<u>after</u> the historical event has been written. This fieldwork is intended as a knowledge-making practice;

- <u>Immersion</u>- Fieldwork involves participation, not merely observation or recording; and
- <u>Identity</u>- We must become one with the past, not a detached observer from the present. Our role in the field must involve context and resonance with particular individuals and specific cultural beliefs.

This makes connection, recovery, <u>and</u> communication a possibility, and not a "hunt". Fieldwork becomes embodied ethnographies of cultural practices that negotiate afterlife biographical fragments. This is a focus, an intervention within particular aspects of the past that have been ignored by historians, conventional archaeological fieldwork, and current paranormal investigations.

Our archaeological work in a "ghost excavation" is the relationship one <u>maintains</u> with a past that is not completed. It works because of a personal mediation (a "direct encounter") between the archaeologist and what remains. The past, however, as it was or as it experienced is an illusionary concept. What remains (after an event has passed), be it a material object, a physical presence, a sensory element, or a memory is only a fragment. It is a partial rendering of what occurred in the past, and of those who performed particular acts.

What remains from the past is a reduction of a seemingly multi-layered cultural world. What remains becomes a finite world of contextual "signs" of presence that were involved in a particular production of space. Anthropologist Tim Ingold, in *The Perception of the Environment (2000)* has said:

"A place owes its character to the experiences it affords to those who spend time there – to the sights, sounds, and indeed smells that constitute its specific ambience. And these, in turn, depend on the kinds of activities in which its inhabitants engage" (2000:192).

That this production is reduced in the archaeological record is normal. It is part of the transformational process of "this happened here" and "this remains" of what happened there. Are these remains any different, or is the experience of excavation so different, from what occurs in a haunting? I think not! The archaeological record of past presence at a haunted location is similarly restricted. That it is does eliminate the need to call the experience a paranormal event!

The active process of interpreting these remaining fragments and traces of continuing past presence is the fieldwork that is involved in a "ghost excavation". In the field (and <u>not</u> in the post-field analysis), we attempt to clarify or understand the meaning and significance of these trace elements and fragmentary manifestations of cultural behavior.

This understanding is also about performance, the acting out of cultural scenarios to "flesh-out" the past, and to give it an intelligible life and context. In the field, we choose to perform some cultural situations that are culturally relevant to the social world of particular individuals who once occupied specific spaces, and were involved in specific situations, at a particular time in the past.

This is an attempt to be accountable for what remains of a more complete past world view and its cultural expressions. This allows us to control our perceptions of what remains, while still in the field. As Henri Bergson states:

"There is no perception which is not full of memories....what you have to explain....is not how perception arises, but how it is limited...."

We limit our field perceptions through the design of particular cultural scenarios. These are based on what occurred in particular spaces, situations, and events at particular times in the past. Our examination of a particular haunted location does not begin with an analysis of prior subjective experiences that were made at the location. We are not there to "debunk" or "authenticate" what has been experienced in the past at these perceived haunted locations.

We choose sites that have little or no "ghost hunting" activity for our "ghost excavations", not approaching it from the perspective of "this happens here". Rather, we focus on "what remains" from a particular moment in time. This involves acts of past production that have created particular performances, experiences, and memories.

The concept of presence is critical. Being "present" is <u>always</u> a sense of construction. What remains is an important part of that construction:

"Traces must be in some way related to social realities" (Ian Hodder, archaeologist, 1978).

This presence, if there are remains, is perhaps "buried" underneath various surface layers of more contemporaneous remains. We must "dig" down to "unearth" it, in context. In a "ghost excavation", this does not involve a physical extraction from the ground.

The investigator, in a "ghost excavation", becomes a "tool" and his/her participatory practices animate, I propose, past presence through cultural resonance (the "awakening" of a past memory field of action). These performance acts "invite" (not "provoke") the flow of communication between past and present.

In a "ghost excavation", we don't wait and then "create" presence <u>after </u>the event of fieldwork has been completed. The manifestations that we recover must be <u>isochronous</u> (simultaneous) to our contextual space-specific cultural scenario. If there is no "response", we move on to the next scenario. We don't "create" a presence in absence ("after" the event of fieldwork). We "recover" this presence in "real time"!

Let's end the "life of ghosts" as "paranormal anomalies", and make them human again. This we can do through our research, and through our performance practices in the field, learning from the experience what it is like to <u>remain</u> human even after the physical death of the body.

Photo 10: The Cultural Scenario as a "Tool" of Research

Investigators Mary Becker (left) and Kathy Rothenberger (right), Gettysburg, Pennsylvania

The Poetics

My use of the word "poetics" in a book about the archaeology of a haunted location is no mere page filler. It is hauntingly appropriate, and archaeologically sensible. An archaeological excavation is a transformative process. Done correctly, it is poetry in motion. A haunting is a choice made that involves an individual, a place, and a social act or event. So too, archaeological excavations involve people, spaces, and acts or performances. A haunting, the excavation, and poetry are all mediators, windows to a particular landscape and its sensual nature:

- A poem, like those penned by Irish poet, the late Seamus Heaney, digs deep through intimate layers of personal memory to unearth and bring to the surface some trace of past presence;
- An excavation recovers the remains of past memory practices, once buried in the ground and perhaps forgotten, that now

surface through the performance practices archaeologists enact in their fieldwork; and

- A haunting manifests in contemporary space as a form of social memory of things **"usually forgotten, discarded, or repressed....about how senses of the past and of place are apprehended and created...." (Richardson 2003:3).**

What unites these three processes (poetics, excavation, haunting) is a particular kind of archaeological sensitivity. A "ghost excavation", through participatory and performance-based cultural acts, stimulate past memories, allowing them to surface (or manifest) in the present as the remains of past cultural presence. The "ghost excavation" becomes an exchange between two entities across space and time. In that encounter, a "common ground", an archaeological poetics is created.

Such a sense of "relational poetics" between archaeology and a haunted location can be found in the poetry of the late Seamus Heaney, manifesting in such poems as "Tollund Man", "The Spirit Level", and as he converses with the dead in "Station Island". In Heaney's poetry, the ghosts become the bodies in the bog, capable of being recovered and significant today.

The haunted record, like its archaeological counterpart, is not a distorted view of history. It is as Richardson, in her book *Possessions: The History and Uses of Haunting in the Hudson Valley,* (2003) states:

"Ghosts operate as a particular, and peculiar, kind of social memory, an alternate form of history-making in which things usually forgotten, discarded, or repressed become foregrounded...." (2003:3).

This "discarded" presence is a major part of the archaeological record during the excavation process. Its significance even forms the title of a popular book on archaeology: *Archaeology is Rubbish* (2002) by Tony Robinson and the late Mick Aston of the popular British TV series *Time Team.* Like the archaeological record, the haunted record of a place contains traces of past cultural memory practices. So we (both in archaeology and ghost research) must work with what remains of that past, even when what we "unearth" is called "rubbish"!

Christine A. Finn, Oxford University archaeologist, has expressed a similar poetic stance to what remains of the past:

"a poetic interpretation of archaeology....one that moves into the metaphysical to consider the essence of a "thing" – should be included in the armory of interpretive tools available to the archaeologist" (2003:74).

In a "ghost excavation", we use "triggers" (music, narrative, poetry, "soundmarks") to take us back in time to become "witnesses" to a still active past, and to bring those still "active" forward in time. Similarly, Heaney's poetry uses objects, and their imagined narrative and context, to bridge the temporal gap between then and now.

This is a form of animating the previously-perceived inanimate, thus rendering sensible the "ghost" by making the present experience a haunting memory in time. The inanimate body of material remains that is recovered during an "excavation" becomes a sensible, but past, human cultural behavioral expression. Its manifesting presence today is a "sign" of a haunting.

The particular poetics of a ghost excavation involves a process of selection (cultural scenarios which are contextually organized into a "ghost script" which resonates with a particular past cultural production of space). This process is framed by a sensible inter-relationship between the archaeologist, the poet ("bridging" the human qualities of a haunting), and the ghost (responding to a culturally-sensible act that they recognize). The ghost excavation "unearths" responsible behaviors from the past by making them archaeologically feasible (contextual to a particular space/time) and poetically-enduring (a human action).

A "ghost excavation" changes a manifestation from an "anomaly" to a cultural artifact (a "sign" or "gesture") of past human behavior, without asserting "poetic license", since these manifestations are recorded in archaeological context. As an archaeologist, I must not forget that, during the excavation, I form part of a particular ghost story, contextual to a particular site, space, landscape, and cultural tradition.

Archaeologist Cornelius Holtorf has recently written, in a piece called *"Learning from Las Vegas" (2007)*, the following:

"Archaeologists can connect so well with some of the most widespread fantasies, dreams, and desires that people have today....the greatest value of archaeology in society lies in providing people with what they most desire from archaeology: great stories both about the past and about archaeological research".

A "ghost excavation" expands that story to include chapters that have largely remained lost, hidden, or ignored by traditional, academic fieldwork. Haunted locations have many such stories, not only "ghostly" ones. During fieldwork, I seek out patterns by using context. In archaeology, context is everything!

Archaeology is the study of "dead" people, someone that exists today as a fragment (or trace) of what was a more complete human life and "body" of acts. These past presences are only brought to "life" again through context. And it is this context that provides a framework by which a story from the past emerges.

This fieldwork, as a "ghost excavation", is also a story of "what-if's": what if I did this, what else would be unearthed, "who" else would manifest? These "what-if's", however, must be culturally-controlled acts that resonate with the human activity and spatial production, together with specific cultural roles, that occurred at that site. The "ghost story" must match the "archaeological story" ("what" and "who" is unearthed). This is the importance of cultural relativity in fieldwork:

"Traces must be in some way related to social realities" (Ian Hodder, archaeologist, 1978).

Equally important is the process of prediction:

"To establish one's explanations, one must predict things about the archaeological record based on already accepted facts....and then find that these predictions are themselves fulfilled on examination of the record" (Watson 1991:277).

The "what if" (contextual cultural scenario) developed for the ghost excavation must predict what occurred in that specific space in the past, and what ("who") still remains there today, based on the historical and ethnographic records: there are no Roman centurions giving commands to companies of soldiers on an American Civil War battlefield!

What archaeology, and a ghost excavation unearth, is their "story", not ours! And so it begins...........

Photo 11: Ghost Excavations in the Field

Left to right, Investigators Mike Stevenson, James Castle, James McCann in a breaker building, Ashland, Pennsylvania

The Craft

We do not view ghost research as a form of entertainment, or a type of physical science. Rather, it is a craft, created, in a "ghost excavation", as a specific design for exploring particular kinds of layered ethno-archaeological sites, and specific spaces within those sites. This notion of "craft" suggests modes of performance acts directed toward iterative engagements with "what" remains from the past at these sites. These performance acts are designed, as social and mental fields of interaction and communication, to resonate with similar fields in the past (see below).

The past, at least some of it, is not dead and gone. Archaeological excavation has proven that time and again. We cannot assume a disconnected past in our fieldwork at these sites. This past that remains does manifest in more ways than one. We work with what's left of the past as it becomes (remains) present today.

In some cases, it is not "what" but "who" remains. Agency and intention are sometimes recovered in an excavation. Archaeology is the **"discipline of things" (cf. Shanks 2012).** Ghost research, I propose, through the use of an archaeological sensibility, can go <u>beyond</u> "things" to "subjects": the recovery of <u>interactive</u> past presence in the present.

One of the first archaeology book I bought as a boy of about 10 was Sir Mortimer Wheeler's, *Archaeology from the Earth* (1954). It still rests securely in my study. Wheeler insisted that an archaeologist excavates **"not things, but people" (1954:V).** I remembered that, and I have retained the idea in my "ghost excavations" at haunted (and "ruined") locations.

A major objective in our fieldwork is to recover the conscious afterlife of a past individual behind the "ghost". This recovery is not a measurement from an electronic device. It is not an "orb", or another light anomaly. It is now even a "shadow". It certainly is not just a "feeling".

If we believe that "ghosts" are "things" (just measurements or recordings), then there is no need for morality or humanity in ghost research. It becomes unimportant how one acts, dresses, or provokes in the field. But if one considers some "ghosts" as the "apparitions of the dead", then we have a moral responsibility to treat them in a humane way, and to act culturally appropriate. If just one of these "ghosts" was a former human being, it is our responsibility to act appropriately. This is because we don't know "what" or "who" they were at the beginning of fieldwork!

This moral code, and its execution during every investigation at "perceived" or presumed haunted locations, becomes the craft of ghost research. This craft is how we design our fieldwork: with empathy, resonance, and socio-historical context to those "who" may remain in these haunted spaces.

We must reach beyond the "orb", the "ghost box", and the entertainment. These particular "objects" of fieldwork are not subject-centered. They are not situated in human reality. They are part of a "ghost hunt" mentality. They belong to a "paranormal" world, not this world, and certainly not the world of the past.

The nature and craft of a "ghost excavation" design practice is a process of co-habitation with a potential interactive human cultural past. This human past, what remains of it, its haunted nature, is always the outcome of our field performances, if we craft our practices to a particular situation in the past.

The result is not a "paranormal" event, but it is an eventful turn of events. Ghost research should not work with a rule book that is separate from cultural reality and archaeological knowledge of presence. We are part of that world that we seek to explore, experience, and understand. A manifestation in haunted space should not be perceived as "alien" to an investigative practice that was designed to produce it. That production is a craft, the craft of ghost research.

Even within the traces that remain, it is the human being, rather than the "ghost" (or an anomaly) that is recognizable. This is to acknowledge that the investigator, as participant, is situated in that world of the past, and that communication is possible with an interaction on equal terms. That connection, between present and past, is the craft of a "ghost excavation".

The Prequel

Photo 12: Introducing the Field of Inquiry: Preliminary Discussions

Left to right, James McCann, Mike Stevenson, Joseph Andrasi, John Sabol, James Castle, Jason Jarvie

Archaeological practices involve the unearthing of remains from another time. That "other" time is usually known only in a fragmented form, similar to a haunting (which is a partial moment in an individual lifetime). During an excavation, it is the actuality of a continuing past that is recovered. It is not the completed past. A haunting changes that experience: it is the past still present!

Given this archaeological (and haunting) process, how can we truly say that the reality of time and presence is linear and exact, one that progressively moves forward and/or "ends" at a particular time? Technologically-speaking, circumstance, situation, and remains may "retreat" in an excavation, becoming something more basic (such as a habitual act with simple tools or devices).

The remembrance of an act may involve a simple gesture, or a discarded artifact. The memory of this is a process of both remembering something, and forgetting many things. Cultural memory is what manifests as "active" material remains at archaeological sites and haunted locations. As humans, we don't remember everything. In an archaeological site, what remains are traces and vestiges. In a haunting, what manifests are particular acts. This is important. As Henri Bergson has said:

"There is no perception which is not full of memories….what you have to explain….is not how perception arises, but how it is limited…."

In an archaeological explanation, the explanation must be based on what little remains of past occupations of space. In a "ghost excavation" at a haunted location, one must explain not only why so little is manifesting, but <u>also</u> why the manifestations that do occur are specific acts of past cultural behavior!

It is these "particularities" of past presence that must be remembered in both archaeological fieldwork and in a ghost excavation. As an archaeologist (and ghost researcher), I selectively excavate, remembering that we are attempting to unearth someone's selective memories. This links the work of archaeology, the "ghost excavation", the practices of remembrance, and the cultural memories of the past that are still "active" today.

In the field, we remember what we learned (and the prior mistakes we made) through research and experience. We also remember certain characteristics/qualities of particular moments of recovery. This remembrance is centered on material remains and materiality. This participatory action, and the unearthing of this past materiality (including "active" sensory elements), is a remembrance which is evoked (and evokes) a particular memory of a past cultural practice and experience.

If time, memory, and experience were simply a storage unit to playback (or erase), the manifestation of trace remains would be unpredictable. They are not! By following deliberate and controlled field practices, archaeological in nature, we focus on "unearthing" particular cultural acts of memory. These field performances emphasize the sensorial character of memory, and are specific to particular past productions of space (such as the importance of sound on American Civil War battlefields).

We can forget about time (as the remote presence of the past) in the sense of experiencing something. This is because an excavation (including the ghost excavation) recovers a memory that is timeless. Materialized cultural remains involve a co-existence, I propose, of multiple times (past-present-future).

A ghost excavation is not a "hunt" for phantoms or anomalies, but rather the recovery of a "ghostly" presence that has been forgotten (perhaps) at multiple times in the past. Today, archaeology and "ghost excavations" focus on the remains of memory practices. This work involves tremendous effort, meticulous excavation strategies, and un-limited time expended in materially producing mnemonic practices that literally "raise the dead", again!

This archaeological field work, the actuality of doing it, becomes the ethnography of a "ghost culture". It is a meaningful, sympathetic, and immersive "disturbance" of the dead. This anthropology of a "ghost excavation" is no mere scan or measurement. It becomes the reality (often times multiple) of interactions with interactive past presence.

Archaeology (Metaphor and Field Practice)

Sometimes, the past is not just a memory.....or a remembrance. Sometimes, it is not the result of an excavation. There are times when the past makes its presence known at unexpected times, places, and in unannounced spaces. An archaeology in and of the present is not detached from the world. It does not separate itself from the past. It is not a "hunt" for what remains. It works with what and, I propose, "who" is still there.

The archaeological fieldworker is not a disembodied observer, detached from the remains of the past. Rather, s/he is an immersed participant in a "living" (not dead) context. This theoretical stance, part of the **"archaeological imagination" (Shanks 2012)**, effectively eliminates the binary (and arbitrary) distinctions made between past/present, between subject/object, and what is present and what remains absent. Fieldwork is art and science, not merely technology and measurement.

Michael Shanks defines the **"archaeological imagination"** as follows:

"a pervasive set of attitudes towards traces and remains, towards memory, time, and temporality" (2012:25).

This is an archaeology that involves **"stretching archaeological interests in directions inconceivable, or at best marginal, a few decades ago" (Shanks 2012:33).** This includes, I propose, the haunted interactive nature of ruined and abandoned sites. This opens up new possibilities to connect with the past.

This involves the uncanny nature of some sites:

"the ways that the past comes back to haunt the living, the way that places contain their pasts, reminding us of half-forgotten happenings" (Ibid: 90).

This is recognition of the "ghostly" presence of particular sites:

"Ghosts operate as a particular and peculiar kind of social memory, an alternative form

of history-making in which things usually forgotten, discarded, or repressed become foregrounded" (Richardson 2003:3).

This is the work of archaeology: to uncover what lies buried, or forgotten, from the past. The challenge of this archaeological fieldwork **"is to reanimate the past by describing and accounting for experiences that resonate and make sense to people today" (Shanks 2012:139).**

How do we accomplish this? According to Shanks:

"Animating fragments of the past can be said to occur....when archaeologists replicate past processes....and of human experience...." (Ibid: 139).

Sociologist Avery Gordon states:

"If we want to study social life well....we must learn to identify hauntings and reckon with ghosts" (1997:23).

This agrees with Robin Wooffitt's call for a **"sociological parapsychology" (2010):**

"But anomalous experiences, whatever their nature, are inextricably implicated in

precisely the social processes and contexts which cannot be reproduced in laboratory conditions" (2010:73).

This is precisely what we do in a "ghost excavation". Our fieldwork is spatial-specific (relative to a particular past production of space, <u>and</u> culture-specific (relative to a past (ethnographic) culture and <u>its</u> belief system). This type of archaeology, as the science of unearthing the remains of past interactive cultural presence, must become an archaeology about and in the present at sites where these manifestations continue to occur. This is an archaeology that is not limited to "ruins", or thinking in terms of a "dead" and buried past. It becomes archaeology that:

"should also be concerned with the study of contemporary objects and places which are still in operation, which are themselves still actively operating and form part of the assemblage on the surface of the world" (cf. Harrison and Schofield 2010).

This is an archaeology where an "excavation" no longer always means "digging-deep" down into the earth. Past presences at haunted locations are surface remains. Fieldwork becomes a contextual performance that "digs" deep to "unearth" the presences of "who" remains from the past. These are performance ethnographies aimed at particular individuals in a past culture.

It is a re-assembling of our current concept of reality, relative to "what" and "who" is actually past and still present in the form of traces of continuing "personhood". This fieldwork, as a "ghost excavation", becomes a creative engagement in the present with those traces of the past that continue to intervene in the spaces of the contemporary.

This contemporary archaeological (as opposed to "paranormal") trope adds credence to what individuals in history and in different cultures have been sensing and experiencing for centuries. This includes anthropologists working in the field in Non-Western cultures.

There are "voices" out there in spaces at sites that remain lost. These voices are often perceived as "anomalies" or naturally-recurring phenomenon. They form part, I propose, of more complex surface assemblages of past cultural memory practices at these haunted sites.

The purpose of our work, as a "ghost excavation", is to close the ill-perceived standardized distance between a past that continues and a present that often denies the existence of these traces. This fieldwork is about making this active past less anomalous (and less "paranormal"), and by documenting its accessibility as a sensible plane (or surface) of contemporary reality.

Photo 13: Fieldwork Operations at Burnside Bridge, Antietam Battlefield (Maryland)

Investigators Jonathan Williams, Mary Becker, James Castle, Sharpsburg, Maryland

This is re-directing archaeology away from its past, and moving it toward the present as past presence manifests within its boundaries. It is also a move away from the question of "if and what exists" to a focus on "how" we can assemble these remains into distinct memory patterns from specific individuals from the past.

It is proposed that the current situation at these haunted sites is that the present is not disengaged from these past traces and vestiges of particular (and earlier) productions and occupations of these spaces. They remain and, though manifesting sometimes independent of intervention (usually a residual vestige), we need specific participatory cultural acts for them to be recovered in a controlled manner.

A belief system, one that views a mysterious and still hidden past, as distinct from the viewable present, actually contributes to the concept of an "anomaly" and the assigning of a manifestation as a "paranormal event":

"the disciplinary orientation toward concealment, mystery, and revelation is

quite obstructive, for it enhances a belief that the past is entirely separate from the present; is 'somewhere else', that needs to be accessed in a particular way" (Thomas 2004:170).

This perception distorts the reality of these haunted sites. It certainly distorts the field methodology that is used to explore these sites (aka "ghost hunting"), through concepts such as "orbs", "shadows", "vortexes", and measured "readings" of monitored space.

Creative, engaged, contextual, cultural participatory acts are needed in these haunted spaces in which traces and fragments of the past intervene in the present. Such an approach becomes a mutual (not demanding or provoking) interaction with a past presence. As archaeologist Julian Thomas has said:

"The remains of the past are all around us, and we inhabit the past in important ways" (2004:170).

The use of contextual cultural participatory acts is meant to engage specific surface assemblages of memory from particular pasts, and individual biographies. This assemblage of remains is found in association, I propose, with each other in a single <u>cultural</u> context. Their "unearthing" must be approached through a <u>single</u> context of participatory acts.

This relation of assemblage/context is important, as the "surface" of haunted space can become complex. This haunted complex is, I propose, a deflated surface without physical depth. Thus, the surface assemblage could involve a mix of multiple pasts, manifesting as symmetry of presences.

Photo 14: Fieldwork at a Haunted Location

Investigation team at the Brunswick Heritage Museum, Brunswick, Maryland

The haunted location becomes a palimpsest, a surface assemblage of mixed traces (and residual vestiges), representing various past productions and occupations of space. Fieldwork is not a process of retrieval from the depths of buried earth. It becomes a creative process of cultural resonance that interacts, as a social process, on the surface.

Participatory field acts can recover a surface assemblage of a specific past event or habitual act, within the palimpsest of space that contains multiple occupations. The remains are then re-assembled. The re-assemblage is a sorting and ordering of various memory traces, and their organization into a data assortment complex I call a particular "ghost culture". This "ghost culture" represents what remains of a particular layer of a past cultural production of a specific space at a haunted location. It involves a particular horizon of meaning (see below).

As modern-day researchers and fieldworkers, we must intimately involve ourselves with the ordered (and systematic) recovery of multiple past realities (of what remains), layer by layer. We must re-orient ourselves and focus on the present, considering the past **"only when it intrudes in the present" (Rodney Harrison).** One of these intrusions, and the focus of a ghost excavation, is those interactive presences from the past that manifest at contemporary locations that may be "haunted" with remains from the past.

In the past, this "haunted" perspective has been largely neglected by archaeologists. It's time for a change! We must focus on, as Rodney Harrison suggests: **"all of the pasts which are implicated in that present".** This is an interventionist and transformative archaeology that is achieved through particular "excavation" (performance) practices. You just don't survey the surface, and measure/record any anomalies!

Through our knowledge and exploration of the past (cultural, social, and historic), we engender new forms of trans-disciplinary research. This new archaeological trope is the old field of ghost research, re-conceptualized in contemporary archaeological terms.

Photo 15: Exploring Ft. Mississauga (Ontario, Canada) (1813-1855)

John Sabol

Place Attachment

In a "ghost excavation", we focus on attempting to "unearth" an interactive past presence. A haunting that generates purposeful human acts ("interactive") in response to an intervention ("ghost excavation") is a particular production of space that remains from the past. I propose that this "intentionality" in a manifesting presence is the remains of a particular memory that is "attached" to a particular space in time.

Sometimes, however, this attachment is "residual", a "recording" of presence. Sometimes, this "recording" is <u>not</u> the past (but a continuing present). And sometimes, it is <u>not</u> a "dead" act that is recorded, but a "living" one. Is the photograph that we recorded of a "jogger" at Burnside Bridge on the Antietam Battlefield in Maryland an example of these "sometimes" contemporary (or contemporary past) events?

Photo 16: The "Jogger" at Burnside Bridge

A core assumption of this "attachment" (as an "interactive" past presence) is that the apparition and his/her/their "world" remains integrally-intertwined in the form of an afterlife consciousness, though the space in which it occurs may have been physically-altered through time. It is interesting that the Burnside Bridge landscape has <u>not</u> changed physically (to a great extent) since the day of the battle (September 17, 1862). This means that the habitual act of the "jogger" may have effectively suppressed what occurred there in 1862, <u>without</u> an alteration of the physical environment.

Because of this "place attachment", a <u>systematic</u> intervention as a "ghost excavation" must be an "unearthing" of presence and memory **"in situ":** the origin and continued manifestation of an interactive "haunting" has not re-located from its <u>original</u> deposition (position) in space and time. This is important, notwithstanding the possibility of a contemporary unintentional "intervention", such as the habitual acts of a "jogger".

This "origin deposition", at a particular place in space and time, is critical, I propose, to the interpretation of a haunting as an interactive past intentional act. It proposes that the haunting was formed within a particular cultural "deposit" of space/time, and therefore its "excavation" requires an "intervention" that is framed by that specific space-time-culture-biographical matrix:

"Traces must be in some way related to social realities" (Ian Hodder, archaeologist (1978)).

This is especially true in a space that contains habitual, almost ritualistic, behavioral patterns, and even when what occurred prior in that locale was something highly emotional and horrific. Though a bloody and deadly engagement was fought at Burnside Bridge, the manifestation of a "jogger" there was not any different from the social reality of what occurs there today: a "jogging" path on the battlefield. This conforms to the following:

"any activity developed over time (such as a habitual "jog") **engenders a space, and can only attain practical reality or concrete existence** (even as a "recording") **within that space" (Lefebvre 1991:115).**

It's important that these "remains", when they manifest, must conform to the archaeological record, past and contemporary past, of what we know (or what we can verify) occurred or occurs there. This is important in the analysis of meaning of these manifestations:

"To establish one's explanations, one must predict things about the archaeological record based on already accepted facts....and then find that these predictions

are themselves fulfilled on examination of the record" (Watson 1991:277).

There are no English queens roaming the halls of an American haunted house! There are no Roman centurions commanding a regiment of Civil War soldiers on an American battlefield!! And there are no past cultural beings (as a form of afterlife consciousness) who "perform" to the demands and commands of contemporary "ghost hunters" unless those commands and commands are contextual (and resonate) in a particular space to a specific cultural behavior in time!!!

A purposeful haunting manifestation that is not recorded "in situ" must be considered out of context, representing something that does not provide accurate, authentic, or reliable knowledge of an interactive past presence. An "in situ" context means that the haunting has not been "re-located" in historical time and space (English history in American historical space).

How does this concept of "place attachment" and a contextual matrix ("in situ" manifestations) fit the methodology of a "ghost excavation"? First, let's more clearly define this "place attachment". A "place attachment is:

"An interaction of individual bodily routines rooted in a particular environment that may become an important place of interpersonal and communal exchange, meaning, and attachment" (Seamon 2013:12).

Let's relate this concept to an American Civil War battlefield. On these battlefields, soldiers died, performing "routines" learned in pre-battle drill. They died in a particular environment. This setting (the battlefield) involved a personal and communal exchange between opposing combatants.

These individuals, as soldiers, were involved in particular bodily routines meant to insure positive effects and outcome ("victory" in battle). These were communal efforts. The transfer of pre-battle drills, as the execution of specific acts in combat (the "ritual" acts) came together in a particular space and time to produce (as "participants" in these "rituals") a large-scale ritual act called a "place ballet" (on the battlefield).

In most cases, these soldiers died far from "home", and many died without receiving or participating in the proper mourning rituals associated with the "Good Death", an important cultural code of mid-19th c. American Society. Because of this, an incomplete cultural pattern to the "end of life" occurred, resulting in the possibility that many of these soldiers may remain <u>attached</u> to this environment (the battlefield), still waiting to go "home" and/or waiting for the proper rituals of the "Good Death" to be performed for them. They remain "attached" to the battlefield because of the importance of this cultural code of the "Good Death".

Their continued presence on the battlefield "mark-off" nodes of haunted space that define particular meaning, intent, military (cultural) behavior, manifesting "signs" of their "culture of war", and the loss of <u>their</u> cultural code of ritual mourning (the "Good Death").

On these battlefields, this emplacement of continued presence becomes, I propose, a displacement of the "Good Death", leading to haunting phenomenon. This signifies a loss of these important cultural values associated with the "end of life" and the concept of the "Good Death".

This theory of an American Civil War battlefield haunting becomes a **"precissing"** (a reduction) of the wholeness that was the culture of war <u>and</u> the culture of death during the period of the American Civil War. It becomes a reduced relationship (as production) within a particular space (a battlefield), as a site of high emotion, intense violence, and high mortality.

Furthermore, their "performance" as soldiers, learned through drills and executed as a response to particular soundmarks (such as bugle calls; officer commands) also was a reduction of a particular cultural tradition (the "culture of war") in a society which valued particular social norms (the "Good Death").

These social and cultural reductions on the battlefield are important, both to the production of that space, and the possibility of a "place attachment" to it by "dead" soldiers who were never accorded the proper rituals of the "Good Death". As Henri Bergson has said:

"There is no perception which is not full of memories....what you have to explain....is not how perception arises, but how it is limited".

On an American Civil War battlefield, this perceptual limitation is based on the concept of the real possibility of the "end of life" and the importance of the "Good Death". Being a soldier in battle, "culture" was reduced to the ritual acts of the "culture of war" and the possibility of death in that culture. With that "reduction", a soldier reduced how he could attain the "Good Death" in battle. There were limited options, reduced to the situation of combat. This meant that there was a real possibility that the ritual of the "Good Death" would not be achieved in battle, or later (if mortally wounded) in a field hospital!

A battlefield haunting, therefore, is both a reduction of cultural behavior (the "culture of war") and cultural belief (dying the "Good Death"). If the relationship between the two is "lost", then a haunting occurs. The "ghost" or apparition, representing this lost relationship in a particular space (the battlefield where he died) becomes "attached" to that place as a direct result, I propose, of this lost (reduced) connection between cultural behavior and belief.

Sociologist Avery Gordon, in her book *Ghostly Matters: Haunting and the Sociological Imagination* (1998) has said:

"...the ghost or the apparition is the principal form by which something lost or invisible or seemingly not there makes itself known or apparent to us. The ghost makes itself known to us through haunting and pulls us effectively into the structure of feeling of a reality we come to experience as a recognition. Haunting recognition is a special way of knowing what has happened or is happening" (1998:63).

This is again a reduction of perception, a contemporary one, of a battlefield death. What is "lost" is this connection between the "culture of war" and a "Good Death". The result, in some cases, is a haunting. And a "ghost excavation" is a recognition of knowing this lost connection. The purpose, through the excavation process, is the re-connection, through the use of contextual scenarios, the relation between the "culture of war" and what was perceived as a "Good Death".

The experience that led a Civil War soldier to the grave (for many this was an unmarked one) was often horrific and direct. At other times, it was an endurance of suffering. But all these experiences involved an intersection within a cultural context, especially what it meant to die the "Good Death". This was an important complex of social attitudes and beliefs that affected, I propose, "who" remains after the production of battlefield space had ended.

This type of haunting is all about dying far from home, and away from the familiar rituals associated with the "end of life". What might be called the **"technology of memory" (Thomas 1993)**, the landscape as memory of the "culture of war" and the "Good Death", makes the "ghost" possible, and perhaps logical, on these battlefields.

This is <u>not</u> an entertaining thought, nor is it a place to conduct entertaining acts:

"The more we experience what the war was like, the more uncomfortable we should become....and we should be uncomfortable

whenever we catch a glimpse of it" (Gramm 2002:XIV).

The manifestation of battlefield haunting phenomenon becomes the "trace" remains (the reduction) of absence of significant cultural codes in the past. The appearance of these manifestations indicates the potential emergence (aided through the "excavation" process) of a different "ghost story", one that is culture-based, and not a "paranormal" event. This is competing (and compelling) history and reality, and not an alternative one.

The "ghosts" in this context do cultural work: they continue to participate in, reinforce, and exemplify the cultural code of the "Good Death", and how it was lost by soldiers on the battlefield. Thus, an important component of the 19th c. belief structure was curtailed in battle. As this loss continues to manifest today on these battlefields, it shows us, I propose, the extent to which the past still influences our present. It is the recognition of this loss that must govern our fieldwork on these battlefields. These landscapes are not an entertainment venue for "ghost hunting"!

There are <u>still</u> unresolved social and cultural issues that continue to manifest on these battlefields today. They speak of a loss that has not passed from the recent past. They (the soldiers) tell us they are still <u>missing</u>, many far away from family and "home". We must understand this in our fieldwork on these battlefields.

The Civil War battlefield is not inactive because some are still at war. They are not "at home". They remain on those fields, a conflict between the "culture of war" and dying the "Good Death". This makes these battlefields a potential landscape of domestic remembrance: this loss of family and cultural ties, still unresolved 150 years after their physical fight had ended.

Because of this, a Civil War battlefield should never become fields of serenity and peace when these social issues still manifest today. As Kent Gramm states:

"May they mourn, brood, scream, stare, cry, lament; may they growl and mutter; may they implore and regret, regret, regret" **(2002:35).**

With these cultural codes clearly in mind, and our efforts set on recovery not on entertainment, we have been testing this theory during our "ghost excavations" at Burnside Bridge on the Antietam Battlefield in Maryland. Specifically, we have developed various contextual cultural scenarios relative to this cultural code of the "Good Death" (such as letters written by soldiers to loved ones at home; the search for missing soldiers on the battlefield; the use of women, portraying relatives of these men, and/or nurses as "substitute" family members, to name a few). This has resulted in a number of interesting manifestations relative to the enactment of these scenarios (for more information on this, please see Sabol 2012; 2013). We are continuing our fieldwork at Burnside Bridge in 2014 with a greater emphasis on the relationship between space (the K.O.C.O.A. military zones; see Sabol 2009), Inherent Military Probability (the "culture of war"), and various "triggers" that are relative to the "Good Death".

Without some sense of how a Civil War battlefield (and dying there) was "culturally-attuned", there is no way to understand or to determine what remains, and "who" may continue to manifest their loss today. We need context in "digging-deep", not measurements or statistics. This requires a participatory aesthetics rather than a detached observer "attuned" to electronic devices and/or a video monitor. This becomes a difference between a "ghost hunt" and a "ghost excavation"!

Photo 17: Cultural Scenario Enacted at Burnside Bridge (2010)

Left to right, Investigators Bigg Jim Jones, Mary Becker, Rie Sadler

Photo 18: Cultural Scenario Enacted at Burnside Bridge (2011)

*Left to right, Investigators Craig Rupp, Natalie Rose,
John Sabol, Cathy 'Cat' Gasch*

Photo 19: Cultural Scenario Enacted at Burnside Bridge (2012)

Foreground, Investigator Mary Becker; background, Investigators James Castle, Jonathan Williams, Cathy 'Cat' Gasch

The "Ghost Culture"

Archaeologist William Walker, in *"Practice and Non-Human Social Actors: The Afterlife Histories of Witches and Dogs in the American Southwest"* (2008) asks the following question:

"Do material traces of interactions between people and supernatural social actors exist (for example ghosts....spirits)? (2008:137).

He states that **"people and other animate forces (let's call them Spirit People) would be both the creators of traits and cultures composed of clusters of traits" (Ibid: 143).** The key work here is "both": "living" persons and "ghosts" create a "culture", composed of distinct clusters of traits. This "cluster of traits" is what I call a "Ghost Culture" (see Sabol 2008; 2012), and this is what we attempt to "unearth" during a "Ghost Excavation".

This "Ghost Culture" is also a "reduction" of cultural elements (behavior or acts and beliefs). On an American Civil War battlefield, for example, this "Ghost Culture" would contain "traits" ("remains") of both the "culture of war" and the "culture of death" (the "Good Death"), unearthed through the resonance between our contextual cultural scenarios, and the memory fields that remain of a past afterlife consciousness from the American Civil War on these battlefields.

This goal to "unearth" the "Ghost Culture" in haunted landscapes during a "ghost excavation" is a focus on assigning intent to nonhuman (or "ghostly") actors as agents (see Latour 1993:30). This requires the assignment of data usually discussed as part of a particular belief system (such as the belief in "ghosts", "spirits", or a "haunting") and **"putting them back into the social world in the form of actors" (Walker 2008:141).**

Assigning intentionality and agency like this (as the "Ghost Culture") effectively eliminates the imposed boundaries **"between people and things, beliefs and actions, and natural and supernatural realms..." (Ibid: 144).** It also eradicates the need (and indicates the absurdity) of conducting fieldwork as a form of pure entertainment!

It is in the importance of memory, as this "Ghost Culture", that ghost research must be based. Why memory, and not the history of a place?

"Memory ties us to an eternal present, while history is a representation of the past" (Meskell 2008:237).

Memory, I propose, is the "home" of ghost research. It is the basis of a "Ghost Culture". "Home" is where the "Good Death" was framed, and where it is still remembered on the battlefield. Because of memory, some Civil War soldiers still haunt the battlefield. Fieldwork on these Civil War battlefields, as an example, must be grounded in contemporary resonating performance practices that invoke this memory of "Home", and not, for example in those continuously repeated as history (such as historical re-enactments), or in those imitated from TV programming as entertainment!

Fieldwork must become a knowing exploration of particular "Ghost Cultures" within a landscape setting, <u>and</u> between sites. This must follow a particular direction ("digging-deep") to unearth the multiple layers of a particular site, cultural frame by cultural frame. This fieldwork is not a surface instrument scan you locate "anomalies" in surface space.

The direction of research, the theory involved, and the application of methodology in the field, is based on what <u>was</u> already there, the past productions of that particular space. The haunting is a palimpsest of those past productions. This **"knowing search",** to use Heidegger's concept, is what I term a "ghost excavation" into the various "ghost cultures" of a particular haunted location, and its various horizons of meaning.

Horizon of Meaning

Haunted locations are unique (archaeological) sites. They contain not only individual haunted spaces, but also a landscape of patterns of haunting associations. These landscape patterns connect various individual spaces together. For example, on a haunted battlefield (Civil War), these would include non-combat zones tied to cultural codes (a place to rest and think about "home"), and military terrain (such as the K.O.C.O.A.), linked to acoustical and Inherent Military Probability (or I.M.P.) behavioral markers.

These multiple haunted spaces that may dot the landscape create various horizons of meaning, all of which cannot be "excavated", due to time and economic constraints. These horizons of meaning are similar to stratigraphic layers. Unlike physically-defined special layers, however, this haunted layering is a shifting hierarchy, dependent upon particular past productions and contemporary performance investigative practices.

No haunted site (or individual haunted space) is a <u>fixed</u> area of presence and manifesting potential. This is because the fragments of all past actions are contained within, and contemporary acts, subject to ongoing acts of behavior, form this layered stratigraphy, as part of these horizons of meaning. Since the present is not past, the future remains fluid (under ordinary circumstances of fieldwork and occupation).

A "ghost excavation", however, changes the flow of potential manifesting presence. By focusing on particular contexts (spatial, temporal, and cultural), the potential for "what" and "who" manifests is <u>intentionally</u> aimed at reducing a seemingly multi-layered cultural world to a manageable and controlled finite world of contextual "signs" (or manifestations) that were involved in a particular past production of space.

The horizons of meaning or strata are "excavated" individually, and perceived from the POV of the present, but the remains of "other" past productions still exist as <u>potential </u>resonances for future "excavating" performances. These "other" horizons are not erased, though they can become suppressed by continuing non-contextual acts from the present (such as those that occur through "ghost tourism" and large "para-celebrity" events and "hunts").

There is no <u>exact</u> time frame, or rigid sequencing of events (such as historical cause and effect) in haunted space, except the one that manifests, however fleetingly, at the moment of perception and recording. But without an "excavating" framework, there is usually no way to ascertain the horizon of meaning that may be manifesting. These uncontrolled manifestations may be due to chance, to provocation, to intimidation, or to some other <u>non-contextual </u>factor. These are non-"in situ" manifestations.

Space, haunted or otherwise, is a material dimension. By occupying it, no matter how infrequent or fleetingly this occupation is, one produces and transforms the space:

"Archaeological remains are inseparable from our present....More deeply still, we are ourselves producers of archaeological materials. We do little more than add a new archaeological episode to the existence of places and things that have often already

known a long series of functions and uses....We add new strata of information...." (Olivier 2001:180).

We must, therefore, be careful in our fieldwork operations. What we may be perceiving in these manifestations may not be the dead "ghosts" of the past, but rather the living "phantoms" of the present. Anthropologist Tim Ingold, in *The Perception of the Environment* (2000), makes an important point:

"A place owes its character to the experiences it affords to those who spend time there – to the sights, sounds, and indeed smells that constitute its specific ambience. And these, in turn, depend on the kinds of activities in which its inhabitants engage" (2000:192).

What are we really encountering at a perceived haunted location? What "ambiances" have been recorded upon that particular environment? Is it a haunting from the past by an active presence; or is it a haunting of the present, as a residual of someone who is still alive? A main objective of a "ghost excavation" is to determine these differences in these multiple horizons of meaning at a site.

The "excavation" of these horizons of meaning that were produced at a location, as a depository (or palimpsest) of acts and resonances restores the cultural integrity of the site in the present, rather that re-iterating the place as something historically eventful in the past. A "ghost excavation" seeks to maintain this cultural heritage, as a remembrance of past productions, for future generations. And the memory of these presences, as a remembrance of "what happened here" becomes more than mere entertainment. This is because "this happened here" then, and this is what remains here now!

Representation and Communication

We live in a world where "normally" there would be no inter-personal, cross-cultural, or actual communication between entities without a system of "signs" that express meaning. This idea is not something beyond reality, present or past. When communication does occur at a haunted location, it does not signify a "paranormal" event has occurred. Communication does occur there, but that communication has remained largely ineffective. Why?

I propose, as a working theory (that is a core concept of a "ghost excavation"), that non-responding and/or missed communication at a haunted location is a result of a misrepresentation by contemporary "ghost hunters", perhaps even by a majority of "paranormal investigators". The basis of this misrepresentation is largely two-fold:

- A lack of <u>identity:</u> The typical "ghost hunt" misrepresents their identity by acting like someone "other" than those who may remain at these sites. Their actions and behavior are not, for the most part, culturally or historically sound. They are out of context with "what" and "who" may remain as residual <u>and</u> interactive past presence. This leads to a second problem that is involved in misrepresentation;

- A lack of <u>immersive participation:</u> Contemporary investigations at haunted locations are little (or poorly) versed in representing those they intend to investigate. This is a problem of a lack of immersive acts (the experience of past situations, not its re-enactment), and a dependence upon observation, albeit involving technology, and <u>not</u> participation.

At the heart of communication (especially at haunted sites) are **shared meanings** between people. We can't merely vocalize questions ("Is anyone here with us tonight?"), or ask, no matter how politely, someone (not "visibly" present) to do something ("Can you show us a sign of your presence?"), especially with a device unknown at the time of the haunting ("Can you turn the meter lights on?"), <u>and</u> expect a communicative response! These acts do not establish a specific "identity" or a particular socio-cultural/historical "context" with which to <u>share</u> these meanings!

Instead, we must <u>create</u> meaning that represents what people (the past presences) thought, and how they acted <u>in the past</u>. In a "ghost excavation", we do this....and more. We also do it, layer by layer, as we "excavate" each horizon of meaning that exists (or potentially exists) at a haunted location.

This has the objective of diminishing the confusion between multiple layers of presence, when one uses one means of behavior for different cultural experiences that may exist and manifest at these sites. The goal is to become contextually representative, and not be uniform in our field practices, as these potential presences attempt to understand our words and behaviors (as "true" representations or "signs" of <u>their</u> world).

A "ghost excavation" involves a specific form of communication, representing various pasts at a haunted site. This is a theory of meaning that includes contextual cultural "signs" (our cultural scenarios), and the execution of these "signs" as a form of communication. This establishes a particular "identity" for us, a solid baseline that is needed in communicating with presence at a haunted location.

Photo 20: Establishing "Identity"

Investigators dressed in period clothing, from different eras, at an alleged haunted site.

Memory

"The terrible gift that the dead make to the living is that of sight, which is to say foreknowledge; in return, they demand memory, which is to say acknowledgement".

- **L. Sante,** *Evidence* (1992)

Once upon a time, there was nothing to remember. Experience had no basis for uncertainty. Past presence did not exist. There was no memory of a history. Ghosts cannot linger long without the memory of something. A haunting memory becomes a history lesson from a remembrance of the past. It comes from the experience of part of the ghost's story.

A "ghosting" of the past in particular spaces become potential modes of communication. A "ghost excavation" is the "unearthing" of a series of scenes within these "ghost stories", of something remembered, and their trajectories through time to the present. They become nodes of presence, a "S.I.M.S." (Sensory Information Memory Setting).

Michael Shanks, archaeologist, once wrote:

"In the archaeological theatre, the discovered past is the play and archaeologists the actors who work on the text producing a performance" **(1991:81).**

This performance, in the field at haunted locations (a "ghost excavation"), releases some meaning of the past toward an audience whose memory is re-awakened. Significance is created because the various images and acts, within that performance, as "signs", resonate to a past experienced (and remembered) haunting moment in time. This significance is a resonance, and this resonance is what precipitates what manifests during a "ghost excavation".

Walter Benjamin, in his *"Berlin Chronicle"*, wrote the following:

"Memory is not an instrument for exploring the past, but its theatre. It is the medium of past experience....".

Memory, within the archaeological chapter of a ghost's story, functions as a representation of particular emotions. This memory field is situational. Certain behaviors in particular spaces represent areas that generate a memory of emotions, perceptions, and experiences. This is why context and resonance are important in any "ghost excavation" at a location haunted by past presence.

But what kind of memory are we talking about in a haunting? Nora (1989) contrasts living memory (playing an active role in the present) with dead memory (existing as detached knowledge about the past). Dead memory revolves around sites in memory as places where events and/or acts occurred that are still not complete (or completed).

In contrast, living memory are environments of memory (such as places where re-enactments are performed) in which the past is continuous (or similar) to the present. Sites of dead memory are the locations where "ghost excavations" occur. These are sites with lost or forgotten, incomplete histories.

In a "ghost excavation", we metaphorically "dig down" (and deep), and not just to recover a past. We also want to "unearth" the participation of a past presence still performing a particular role in the past, one that has been remembered. And one that has been recalled, in memory, through our field performance practices.

Ghost research, as that fieldwork dealing with interactive manifestations and apparitional experiences, is the study of past memory, not a location's history, not even its "haunted" history. Historical accounts are themselves fragmented "ghosts" of what happened in the past.

They are also potentially a misrepresentation (because of partiality and bias) of what occurred (and certainly what continues) at a site (and in particular spaces). A "ghost" is a different type of "historian". S/he has a different version (and access) to the memory traces of a place. These memory traces are created and develop within particular groups. The behavioral practices (and memories of experiences) that ensue create a social bond, a sense of belonging, a place attachment, and a cultural identity.

Buried memories are an archaeological journey into the world of socio-cultural and historical presences. They contain haunting remains of a fragmented past. They contain a series of spaces that enact the effects of multiple uncertainties. There are "ghosts" in these landscapes in memory. They belong to a different time and place that once existed in these haunted spaces.

These "ghosts" are real. They are not phantom presences. Their manifesting memories haunt the ruined spaces that inhabit sites of remembrances of past productions of space. That they exist in reality is why we conduct our "ghost excavations" there!

Photo 21: What Memories Still Remain of this Past Production of Space?

Investigators in the field at these haunted locations must enter the social world of the "ghost". Identity must be established through cultural acts. A rapport between investigator and "ghost" must become a shared experience and understanding of past cultural reality that becomes, with interaction and communication, a common memory. These manifestations of past acts are "still points" of memory that maintain the same reality (to the "ghost") as it was in the past.

Like a recall of memory, a "ghost excavation" is a re-collection and remembrance of past events, acts, experiences, and people. It involves a recovery, sometimes deep within the soiled deposits of a mind fragmented into pieces from the past. These memories are converted, I propose, into physical forms that carry significance into the present.

Past manifestations percolate in symmetry at haunted sites to a present experienced moment in the field. This is both the performed act of a past memory, and a contemporary performance meant to "unearth" it. This produces a future stage that shows what became of those past and present performances.

Haunting manifestations bridge multiple times by unfolding them into the present. This is not history. It is memory, where a past remembrance becomes a present moment. Ghost research is a mediated process between an academic recognition of this past presence (archaeology), an immersion into cultural practices and rituals (ethnography), and resonating and contextual acts that "ghost" those past memory fields ("ghost excavation").

A haunting resists the re-inventions and re-engagements of space, place, culture, and technology. The "remains" of cultural memory left in a haunting can become themselves merely a "memory", without contextual and resonating intervention. Without cultural acts that can be used to recall those former memories, certain histories and stories of the past can become lost and forgotten. This is what happens when technology becomes the "ghosting" of past memories!

Still, what becomes of the archaeologist who narrows the search for past presence, concentrating his efforts on the continuing <u>interactive</u> presence of the past at haunted locations? What if this "dig" begins and ends in (with) memory? Does that change the significance of the excavation? Does it alter the remains that are recovered, or the analysis and significance of those remains?

Howard Carter, the noted Egyptologist, once said:

"a heavy weight of responsibility must at all times rest upon the excavator" (Carter and Mace 1977:125).

The memory of this responsibility is recalled each and every time we conduct a "ghost excavation"!

The fundamental proposition of archaeological work (and ghost research, I propose) is that we can explore and study only the remains which survive from the past. This is not a complete record of the past, or what occurred in a specific space during a particular occupation of that space. What does survive, even in this fragmented form, is human cultural behaviors and cultural expressions of those past occupations.

It is not a paranormal event, an inhuman entity, or supernatural acts achieved after death. It is also not "orbs", "ghost box" transmissions, or most other anomalies. What remains from the past survives only because the world has changed (Olivier 2008:267).

The archaeological record of a haunted space should be perceived, not as forms of "evidence" to be recorded and measured, but as "signs" (sensory manifesting elements) of particular memories. These remains involve the processes of recognition, recall, repetition, and transformation, as whole patterns of cultural behavior revert to vestiges and traces.

It is this transformation that allows us to make sense of what remains in the archaeological record. These past presences are human remains, and are not "paranormal" in nature. They are past memory practices, and not "anomalies". They are life events of human individuals, and not supernatural behaviors of non-human entities.

Experiential Fieldwork

A "ghost excavation" goes beyond simple descriptions of field experience, and/or measured deviations in the physical environment. It is intended to "unearth" and recover, eventually understand and explain these manifesting past cultural performances. In a "ghost excavation", a manifestation represents, I propose, the completion (an intentional "sign") of the cultural expression of a past memory that is embedded in a particular role and identity.

This element of presence is not haphazard. It is intentional. It represents cultural behavior, not a physical law. This is because:

- Haunting manifestations are "cooked". They are not a random, "raw" anomaly. They are "signs" of an intentionally-understandable (not "paranormal") past cultural act;
- Haunting manifestations are basic modes of human interaction and communication. They are not manifestations of a

"supernatural" ability a "ghost" or "apparition" acquires after physical death;

- Haunting manifestations are socially co-created through contextual culturally-resonating interactions. They are not acts that are performed by beings whose identities are completely unknown (at least not in a "ghost excavation");
- Haunting manifestations are "effective" acts. They are understandable communicative responses;
- Haunting manifestations are "emergent". This "becoming" present resides in the interplay between contemporary immersion and participatory acts, investigative competence (or research skill), and the contextual resonance of the cultural scenario that is enacted; and
- Haunting manifestations are not always successful. We are dealing with human behavior, individual cultural and psychological codes of "likes" and "dislikes". This also means that the level of ethnographic immersion (the resonance of a particular cultural scenario to a specific past

act of behavior) remains a deciding factor in communication. There are no "guarantees" that an interactive past presence will emerge during field performances.

A "ghost excavation" involves experiential learning. Research continues in the field through a ethnographic process of participation-observation in a past cultural setting that may be characterized as the presences of past cultural beings who are enacting (performing) traces of their social practices ("ghost culture") in particular spaces at a haunted location.

In this type of fieldwork, the investigator becomes an ethnographer by virtue of the adoption of a particular kind of perspective (immersive, participatory, and empathetic), within the archaeologically-related process of "digging-up" presences by layers of cultural occupation.

This is a view of a haunted location as an archaeological site, and recognizing this site as an important space of social production <u>and</u> potential future re-emergence. It is a view of a haunted site as "**historically produced social spaces**" and as **"active, dynamic, contingent spaces of**

the production of social relations" (Breglia 2006:7).

A "ghost excavation" involves thrice-behaved experiential behavior within this re-production of social space and relations:

- The immersion of the investigator into a particular horizon of meaning at a haunted location;
- The "targeted" performance (cultural scenario) that is aimed at a particular afterlife conscious mind in a specific cultural situation; and
- The cultural response or communicative intent by the "ghost" or "apparition" to the "targeted" performance.

The "ghost excavation" is a blending of art and science. It is theatrical. But it also involves an iterative process (a "ghosting" of past investigative performances) that can be repeated by other investigators at other times. This is a type of fieldwork than can document repeatable past performance (as experienced), negating, in the process, the concept of haunting unpredictability.

The process itself is experiential. It is felt, and that feeling is acted upon through the use of contextual cultural scenarios. The use of these resonating acts in the field is the quickest, most constructive (and easiest) means, I propose, to "project" a specific contextual "identity" to the past presence. It is this contextual "identity" that allows interaction and communication to occur between the investigator and specific interactive past cultural presences.

"P.O.P." (Participate-Observe-Perform)

At haunted locations, I have been using the "P.O.P" for more than three decades now. Recently, I have seen a similar approach being used by other field investigators, including some on "Paranormal TV". Interestingly, I know all of these investigators, have openly talked to them (some quite extensively) about my field methodology, and even given them examples of its application in the field. Coincidence? That is a discussion for another time and place!

The question to be discussed here is this: what and where are "living" archaeological sites? Are there really places where events/past acts "still occur"? If so, can these manifestations be "unearthed" in a "controlled" excavation? If actual present reality is more than the nexus of the past and future, and if there is the real possibility of a continued "life" after death, can we purposely "activate" that past?

Is it possible to enable (or predict) a future for these currently haunted locations, one that will stand the test of time and abuse (or provocation) that is rampant in "ghost hunts" today? Can we enable this future to become an event that is <u>still</u> historically and socially sound with the past? Is there some activity and "someone" still "alive" from the past that can be countenanced (or re-countenanced) in future time?

At haunted locations, a "ghost excavation" can help to dissolve the distinctions between past and present. It's a difference, I propose, between "digging-now" (through immersive performances with "immediate" field reveals) and "monitoring/sweeping" a site for future review. It is participating, observing the effects of that participation, and performing immediately to any communication that manifests as a result of that participatory act (P.O.P.).

Communication with past presence is the degree to which we allow these participatory cultural investigative acts, and a responding (intentional) past performance to those acts, to be seriously considered in field research. If we grant importance to this consideration, then, I propose, a future interactive manifestation, using the same (or similar resonating cultural acts) becomes a distinct possibility.

How is this possible? How can past, present, and future occur in the <u>same</u> space, separated only by the moments between contemporary participatory acts, a manifesting past "response", its observation, and a continuing performance that responds to that past act? This is accomplished through a "live" participatory act, in an immersive situation, that resonates with a memory field of a particular horizon of meaning, recalled <u>and</u> accepted by a particular past presence. This is because, I propose, <u>our</u> "identity" (as one of <u>them</u>) has been accepted.

Performances are always reiterative, even more so as haunting manifestations. They are a "theatrical ghosting" of past performances by both "dead" and "live" actors. These are sensual forms of "unearthed" remains from the past (perhaps multiple pasts) to the present, <u>and</u> continuing into the future.

P.O.P. is one way, albeit a contextual way, that social histories and memories are captured in ethnographic context. That recovery of a past cultural expression or "sign" is time sensitive. They occur, in most instances, immediately after a contemporary scenario has been enacted. The manifestation, therefore, belongs now (the present), and is not just confined to the past. But this temporality is distinct from evolutionary time, cultural development, and technological advancement.

These performances, within a theatre of memory and using an ethnographic-inspired methodology (P.O.P.), are an archaeological look (and sensitivity) that systematically attempts to recover a hidden (or lost) cultural history and individual presence. It is a means of using the "tools" of the body (as experiential experience) as a means of accessing the past. It is also a way in bridging what is a past, becoming present, that can continue into the future. It is a way to "P.O.P." the popular notion of space, time, and reality.

For more information of the "P.O.P." methodology, with its theoretical background (and examples of its use in the field), please reference my book on the subject, *Digging Up Ghosts* (2012).

Photo 22: Using the P.O.P. Method in Fieldwork

Investigators at an alleged haunted site

Photo 23: Another Example of Using P.O.P.

Investigator Mike Stevenson

The "Ghost Script" and "Haunting Storyboards"

Performance and theatrical productions contain the same ritualistic-like elements as the participatory acts that we enact in a "ghost excavation". This symmetry between the two can also be called what Rupert Sheldrake has termed **"morphic resonance" (1981).** This is **"a process whereby the forms of previous systems influence the morphogenesis of subsequent similar systems...." (1981:84).**

Theatrical productions and investigative field performances are social events between a performer (or social actor) and a "targeted" audience. They usually occur within a specific physical space and context. The performance usually (but not always) takes place at night, and in the dark. There is a real sense of mutual presence, though it is largely "unseen".

The performance is focused and purposeful. Non-living entities and past events are invoked. Intense concentration is required, and high emotion is transmitted and felt. Finally, there is a concerted attempt at establishing a communicative link between the authenticity of the actor's performance (establishing an "identity"), and the personal (and sometimes individual) experiences (and memory) of the "targeted" audience.

Communication and social interaction (together with <u>mutual</u> identity) is established when the contemporary cultural scenario creates a resonance with those of the past (as a form of "morphic resonance"). This social interaction is achieved because these immersive, and resonating, contemporary acts are focused on behaviors and situations of shared experiences, recalled in memory.

The participants (both present and past), and their mutual intent and understanding, are co-equally communicated through the resonating quality of a "ghost script", framed by a series of contextual cultural scenarios that follow a common (past) theme ("haunting storyboard"). This creates a direct field of cultural resonance, what Sheldrake calls a **"morphogenetic field" (1981:85):**

"Morphic resonance takes place through morphogenetic fields and indeed gives rise to their characteristic structures. Not only does a specific morphogenetic field influence the form of a system....., but also the form of this system influences the morphogenetic field and through it becomes present to subsequent similar systems" **(Ibid: 85-86).**

The enactment of a "ghost script", derived from a "storyboard" based on what occurred in a particular space, with specific individuals, at a particular point in history, and using specific cultural situations and experiences, stimulates (like the **"morphogenetic field"**) a similar response from this past event. It is a recovery of the "ghosts" from the past that are still active within that past system.

Field performance (cultural and resonating), a principal component in a "ghost excavation", is an important "key" to unlocking the door to the past. The use of cultural scenarios (the "ghost script"), based on a particular past "storyboard", is a direct (and personal) invitation toward the entities that may remain to participate in cultural acts and situations that they themselves are fully aware of, having experienced them during their lifetimes.

This "ghost script" is composed of four basic elements:

- **Ideological Component:** This is composed of the underlying cultural codes of the horizon of meaning that is to be "excavated". For example, if we are investigating a American Civil War battlefield, these cultural codes would include the "culture of war" of that period (Inherent Military Probability or I.M.P. behaviors: how the soldier would have acted/what he would have experienced in pre-battle, during combat, and when wounded or dying; K.O.C.O.A. military space; the concept of a "band of brothers"); the "culture of death" of mid-19th c. America (the "Good Death"; "domestic imagery", or the importance of "home" and family);
- **Structural Component:** This involves organizing these cultural codes into a series

of contextual behaviors and "triggers" (for example: "soundmarks" on a Civil War battlefield) tied to particular battlefield spaces (the K.O.C.O.A.);

- **Sensory Component:** This is the use of auditory, visual, olfactory, and gustatory (contextual) cues relative to the ideological component; and the

- **Transactional Component:** This is the actual "storyboard" of scenarios, as it will be "acted-out" in the field, with spatial and temporal components firmly in place. For example, on a Civil War battlefield, this would follow a particular battle's movement and flow through the K.O.C.O.A. spaces, as it would have occurred and described in the historical record.

This "script" and "storyboard" includes a thorough social and historical knowledge of each role, and participatory practice, to be enacted in the field: they must be contextual and ethnographically-sound. This insures the proper "identity formation".

It also involves such acting techniques as "targeted" pauses, silent contemplative moments, shouts and commands (when contextual), non-verbal cues, use of specific grammar, vocabulary and slang words, voice tone and pitch, and "interpretive" tools (such as costuming and personal items). It does matter "who" is the person that is performing the scenario. For example, on a Civil War battlefield, woman would not participate in the combat scenarios, unless women (in the role of men) actually fought in that particular battle.

Age is another important consideration, and the role a particular age group enacted in that situation in the past (for example, the drumming in a Civil War company was enacted, in most cases, by young boys, as opposed to mature adults). All of these are important considerations in the writing of the "ghost script", its purpose to firmly to establish a specific, and contextual, "identity".

If "ghosts", and their contextual matrixes (associations between beliefs, acts, experiences, spaces, and sensory elements) are potential interactive fields of surface remains, we need to utilize all of our field practices (as contextual performance roles) to recover their remains. Only then can we begin to communicate and interact with them, as they remember interactions in <u>their</u> world.

Summary

The power and excitement of archaeological fieldwork lies in its ability to recover some aspect of the past. Excavation grants us access; however fragmented this may be, to worlds and peoples which cannot be apprehended by any other means. This is a constructive and significant baseline to explore that "other" world of haunted space.

As field investigators, we can situate ourselves in relation to past presence in a variety of ethnographic ways, once we begin to "excavate" each of these worlds, one level (or horizon of meaning) at a time. It is the very absence of data encountered in archaeology, however, that we can utilized and expand the field of ghost research. We can bring creative thinking into our acts and performances in the field.

The haunting quality of archaeological and ethnographic work is not total absence, but the presence of remains and cultural expressions that indicate, and draw attention to, a presence that is not past: this is what is left after the act, the event, and the ritual. But, and here is where ghost research comes into play: is that really all that remains? What more may remain and how can we make contact, and communicate after (or during) the performance of excavation?

The excavation, itself, is a re-occupation of the site and its spaces. Therefore, it becomes critical how this excavation occurs, so as not to contaminate "what" (and perhaps "who") remains. This fieldwork is a negotiation of space in which the investigator acquires, with time, a familiarity with the place and its presences through engagement and the performance practices.

Fieldwork should not be a passive one, dictated by the "work" of electronic instruments which control contemporary behaviors. The excavation of haunted space is much more inclusive than the use and observation of meters and electronic devices. Working in haunted space, as an archaeological site, one can find oneself amongst other (previous) occupations.

"What" and "who" remains is a re-animation by contemporary <u>human</u> agency, not an instrument. Curiosity "killed the cat". It does not re-animate the dead (unless it is a "ghost cat"). Familiarity beckons memory, which stimulates the possibility of presence. This familiarity, in a manner and tone that resonates with past acts in a particular space, is what we use (have used for decades) to recover the presences that might remain after a particular occupation.

When a presence is drawn into the present by a familiar (and contextual) act, it can be deeply felt, even if it relates to a different time and particular place attachment beyond the investigator's personal knowledge and experience. This contemporary "apparitional experience" is not a "constructed" memory. It is, rather an <u>enacted</u> one.

Ghost research must re-consider the notion of "presence" at haunted locations. There must be a recognition of the human behind the haunting. Manifestations are not mere "objects" or measured deviations. They are, I propose, conscious memories that occupy a particular niche in a cultural ecology of space and time.

A person is <u>not</u> physically bounded by their flesh and blood. A human life (and its "afterlife") of particular memories can stretch over time outside the box of conventional dates. This human memory is made conscious through social interactions and cultural effects, not "bleeps" and "colored lights" from meters!

Presence <u>does</u> linger in absence (both physical and cultural). In order to make these particular presences come to "life", however, we need the prompting of both an archaeological sensibility and an ethnographic sensitivity. This mutual interaction is done in order to know the "signs" of "what" (and "who") to look for: the traces of past occupations of space at haunted sites.

There is also an ethical question to consider, assuming that we consider some of these manifestations were (are) human in origin. We must be responsible adults (and not incorporating children into the field equation) in how we interpret or re-connect with the presences of these "ghosts". Is it unethical to depict such unflattering manifestations of humans (as "ghosts") in the form of "orbs" and "ghost box" transmissions?

The answer goes beyond a simple statement of honesty and interpretation. If it is a human past presence that is manifesting, then this past belongs to no one in the present, representing contemporary "ownership", authority, or accessibility. Past presence is the shared cultural heritage of everyone. That shared heritage must not be exploited for personal gain, motive, or entertaining use!

This then is what remains: is a "haunting" an archive of "what happened here" which made a "ghost" in a specific space at a particular time in the past; or is the past just a "memory", and/or a conscious re-performance by a "dead" individual?

Is a "haunting" a contemporary occupation by "ghost hunting" groups, and their practices, and/or a ghost tour version of a fractured mix of history and folklore? Whatever it is, one thing is certain. What we must recover and document is the former before the intervention of the latter!

The archaeological record has been likened to a memory, a palimpsest of **"memory-objects" (cf. Olivier 2008).** There is a fine balance in the haunted record between preservation and loss, between inscription and erasure, and between what remains (as this archaeological record of "memory-objects"), and how much of this is recoverable, and is recovered as the haunted record of a site.

A haunting, and its investigation, is like that: a fine line betwixt and between the "hunt" and an "excavation" in haunted space. We don't "hunt", but we do "excavate", and this "excavation" requires discipline, control, expertise, and meticulous work.

This "excavation" is not entertainment, a "training ground" for a "ghost hunting" academy, a playground for adults and children, a hobby, or a religious-like pilgrimage, a vocation, or a devotion to something that is considered "paranormal". This is fieldwork, pure and simple! Whether "ghost hunters" like it or not, or believe it or dismiss it, this is serious research!

The fundamental proposition of this archaeological work in ghost research is that we can explore and study only that which "survives" from the past. And what does survive is human cultural behavior. It is not a "paranormal" event. It is not an inhuman entity or a supernatural act. It is also not "orbs", "ghost box" communications, or other so-called "anomalies".

What remains from the past survives only because the world has changed (Olivier 2008:267). The archaeological record, and I propose the haunted record, should be perceived as "signs" or "cultural gestures" of particular memories.

These remain, and can be recorded as manifesting presences, because they involve recognition, recall, repetition, and transformation (as whole patterns to vestiges and traces). It is this transformation that allows us to make sense of these past presences as human, not "paranormal" in nature; as memory practices, and not as "anomalies"; and as "life" events, and not supernatural ones.

Memory, specifically socio-cultural memory, is the key that unlocks the door. It opens contemporary reality to the possibility (even probability) of "other" worlds. The "ghost" becomes an "afterlife conscious mind". An interactive haunting becomes a re-performance of cultural habits and behaviors.

A non-human does not have human memories. A "paranormal" event is <u>beyond</u> the performance of human activity and memory. This is <u>not</u> the case in most hauntings. And it is not the context of perception when a "ghost" is documented as "manifesting" in a "ghost excavation". Memory makes a "ghost" and an "interactive haunting" humane.

The traces and vestiges that materialize in haunted spaces can be defined as a material sensory memory. If these materializations are from the past, they are not past and gone. They are present still, just like past remains are still present which archaeologists "dig-out".

Time becomes irrelevant. A haunting and its ghosts become contemporary cultural phenomenon, yet simultaneously of (from) the past – just like archaeological remains. A "ghost excavation" makes that connection between archaeology as the science of the material remains of past presence, and ghost research as the potential scientific discipline of past interactive presence...

The goal of all "ghost excavations" is the recovery of some trace of the memory of an individual biography from the past. It is a difficult, at times impossible task.

As Loren Eiseley has said:

"A biography is always constructed from ruins but, as any archaeologist will tell you, there is never the means to unearth all the rooms....You try to see what the ruin meant to whoever inhabited it, and if you are lucky, you see a little way backward it time" (1975:217).

At Burnside Bridge, on the Antietam battlefield in Maryland, we have recovered, we believe, some of those traces of the personal biography of Lt. Colonel William Holmes of the 2nd Georgia, and Private Alvin Flint of the 11th Massachusetts. We hope to continue their ongoing story in 2014, with continued "excavations" into their "afterlife" presences on that battlefield.

Photo 24: Alvin Flint

Photo 25: The "Empty" Grave Site of William Holmes

Appendixes

The Haunted Sensorium

In a "ghost excavation", it's all about making sense of past memory practices. Memory is important for ghost research because it reminds us what it is to be human. It is a social, not supernatural, practice that is embedded in the relations people develop with one another (and with particular places); and apparitions develop with contemporary humans, I propose, in particular social contexts.

These social practices also extend to what people did (and continue to do), where they did it, how, and with whom. That is why it is first important, in a "ghost excavation", to establish identity, and then to resonate with "who" may remain through specific cultural activities in particular spaces at a "haunted" site. This becomes the recovery of past memory practices that make up the archaeological record of a particular site.

Thinking about memory and its potential physical traces (as sensory elements) is worthwhile because these remains, as manifestations, are framed within social contexts. As "excavators", we can focus on questions of meaning that are derived from physical or physically-sensed residues of the actions, interactions, and re-actions that produced these memory fields.

The ways through which people (now "ghosts") learned, experienced, and now remember, I propose, were (are) situated in particular social, spatial, temporal, and physical expressive contexts. These contexts must be researched for particular sites, and then become the focus of our ghost research in the field at these haunted locations.

Memories are linked acts of experience that "ghosts" once engaged in through social practices. In a "ghost excavation", we focus on how these "ghosts" interact with the world around them in contexts that are localized in space and time. A relationship between space, time, cultural practice, and memory becomes obvious during the "excavation" process.

In a "ghost excavation", the presence of memory traces form fields of haunting phenomenon, linked together by sensory elements. These linkages provide a means to understand why a particular historical/cultural embedded consciousness remains after the death of the physical body and brain. It also shows how memory is made manifest as a sensory element of a "ghost culture", memory practices that have become embedded and recorded onto particular landscapes.

In a series of essays that follow, I will outline the importance of some of these sensory elements for ghost research as forms of memory fields that are embedded at haunted locations. The importance of these surface assemblages, as they relate to particular past practices, will be discussed.

The Haunting Gesture:

The Codification of

Interactive Presence

In the long, haunted history of ghostly manifestations there has yet to be identified a universally-applicable means to culturally codify this phenomenon. There has been taxonomies of forms (residual, interactive, crisis, etc.), but no social criterion based on context (space and time). As a trained cultural anthropologist, I am concerned with the process of performance in any documented case of presence at a haunted location.

An individual's character and personality traits, and their attitude to what they have experienced in life, can be understood from the objects in which they choose to associate, their personal preferences regarding dress and adornment, and the places and activities where they prefer to inhabit, remember, and continue to perform tasks and habits. This sensual materiality, as "artifact" remains, can be "codified" during a "ghost excavation".

The baseline for this codification, I propose, is cultural performance. Even the most mundane, or habitual, activity involves the use of specific cultural expressions, themselves based on social beliefs typical of that particular society. As the manifesting "expressions" (or "signs") of ghosts vary, from one cultural horizon of meaning to another, so do these sensory elements that accompany their presence.

This is a function, I propose, of societal and individual preferences and norms, and <u>not</u> physical laws. These manifestations are set and embedded in particular historical settings, not just any setting. A manifesting presence (residual or interactive) should not embody the characteristics of a time period other than their own (except perhaps "ghosts" who were actors in life).

The codification of this phenomenon is an archaeology of cultural haunting gestures. It involves a specific research methodology. The documentation of this phenomenon is only possible if the cultural "gesture" (or "sign") leaves an enduring memory trace in the consciousness of the entity, and that trace behavior continues in specific spaces of particular locations.

This manifesting presence, like physical remains at an archaeological site, operates within a particular pattern of "normal" social behavior (for a particular time period and culture). It must be noted that this "normalcy" is not <u>always</u> the case. There are always socially-deviant individuals who do not conform to a society's social norms. If these manifestations occur, it does not mean, however, that they are "paranormal" (only "deviant" for that particular horizon of memory).

The understanding of haunting phenomenon at particular sites necessitates a concern, on the part of all the investigating team, for a research agenda that includes outlining the social structures and social behaviors of the cultural "gestures" (or "signs") of particular time periods (and social spaces) where and when a haunting might occur at a particular location.

These socio-cultural structures and "normal" behaviors contain, I propose, the cultural codes for a particular location, and its potential haunted history. These cultural codes will vary from site to site. They will even vary within a site, dependent upon the quantity of haunting layers that exist as surface assemblages in particular spaces.

The relationship between an <u>interactive</u> past presence, their cultural "gestures", and interactions in the present, is an intimate and empathetic process. It does not (ordinarily) come about through the use of contemporary recording and measuring devices. It does not (ordinarily) occur while "sweeping" an area, or by means of an inactive "watch and wait" field technique.

The "haunting gesture" is a purposeful act that comes to fruition because it is socially and culturally communicative in that (for that) past culture. This cultural "gesture" is not a "light anomaly", a "drop" or "rise" in the temperature, or an elevated (or changed) EMF reading which is <u>not</u> connected to a contextual "cultural gesture" that is typical of a past society's social means of expression.

Alone, these ambient deviations are not measuring cultural performance or recording an intentional act. These measurements and recordings can become significant when they are established (in context), and linked to particular participatory cultural scenarios that resonate with past cultural acts in specific spaces at a site.

The "cultural gesture" is a material act of remembrance, not merely a telepathic projection to someone. The "gesture", I propose, manifests the intentions, feelings, and belief system of the past interactive social presence. Different societies and cultures have different ways of expression. To be in a particular emotional state, one that is remembered (and one that is not necessarily a tragic or traumatic one) is to perceive the world in a particular way. It also affects, I propose, "if" there is a manifestation, and "who" that manifestation is, after physical death.

There is something meaningful in the way we act, and in the manner we interact that can transcend space and time. Alfred Gell (1998) talked about this:

"A person and a person's mind are not confined to particular spatio-temporal coordinates, but consist of a spread of biographical events and memories of events, and a dispersed category of material objects, traces, and leavings, which....during a biographical career....may prolong itself long after biological death" (1998:222).

These personal biographies (or fragments of biographies of an afterlife conscious memory) are based on the cultural codes that are still embedded in memory fields at haunted locations:

"Personal biographies are formed through encounters with particular places in the cultural landscape, and the recognition and understanding of the panoply of codes constituting their meaning" (Tilley 1993:82).

We use these cultural codes to recover personal (but fragmented) biographical memories of past entities in a "ghost excavation".

There is something meaningful in the way we act, and in the manner in which we interact. This does not end for all of us at physical death. "Cultural gestures" matter because they operate within the socio-cultural milieu of the manifesting presence. Their communicative "gesture" (as an intentional response) lies in their capacity to transmit cultural knowledge to us in the present. The nature of this "cultural gesture" identifies it (the manifestation) as coming from a human agent, framed within a particular cultural sphere.

The "cultural gesture" is a transmission of specific (and directed) energy. These energies were expended (are being expended) doing cultural activities, including habitual and mundane tasks. The energy that is dispersed (both past and present) is a function of intended cultural expression.

These gestures, I propose, are disciplined actions, intended to produce a controlled act. The "gesture", when manifesting in unison with a contemporary performance act, is recognition of the link between cognitive processes (memory) and the social environment.

We need to recognize these "cultural gestures" in the field, and to distinguish them from random acts (or manifestations). These <u>are</u> disciplined movements and tasked performances.

The baseline technique for a codification of these "cultural gestures", I propose, is the ritual of participatory cultural contextual scenarios. Ritual, as perceived ethnographically, is largely based on imitation and repetition, as a resonance to what was performed in the past. Its principal feature is the emotional stimulation and immersion of the senses that is involved in the process.

Why should beings use gestures when language is available? For a "ghost", that is a different set of circumstances. If one has no vocal cords, what survives physical death with which one can communicate? Could the memory of "cultural gestures" (as "signs" of an attempt at communication) be the answer? Could the memory of "cultural gestures", as the earliest communicative trait in human social evolution, be the principal type of communication that survives death?

Music is a re-invented gesture. It is a meaningful language for consciousness, in whatever form this may exist. It aids in the recall of memory. It certainly aided soldiers in combat during the American Civil War. Does a contemporary use of music aid in recovering the memories that survive of some of these soldiers on Civil War battlefields? Music has proven to be an effective tool in fieldwork at these locations (cf. Sabol 2012; 2013).

The "cultural gesture" is relative to fieldwork in landscapes, sites, spaces, and in architectural enclosures in which apparitions (or "ghosts") had once lived. These settings and physical features affect the way the "ghost" choreographs their movements in and through the spaces of a haunted location. Those settings and those features become their cultural view of the landscape as "hauntscape".

The archaeology of these "cultural gestures, layered in embedded deposits at a haunted location, can form part of a change in attitude (and latitude) of a more socially-oriented ghost research. While "ghost hunters" continually embrace modern scientific technological devices, the "technology" of thinking, understanding, and explaining the significance of a manifestation lags far behind.

The "thinking" (?) behind a "ghost hunt" is very under-developed, if at all. It is certainly not based on ethnographic research or methodology. And it certainly does not focus on cultural/ethnic diversity. Technological devices measure the same thing. They do not measure "cultural gestures" as "signs" of a particular cultural haunting in diverse contexts and social situations.

Ghost hunting, as a "ghosting" of what most others do (without regard to cultural/environmental diversity), is largely based on "describing" (in mostly subjective terms and/or measurements) the investigation of a haunted site. During a "ghost excavation", we consider it far more significant to think about the potentially diverse cultural dynamics of a haunted site.

Ghost hunting, at its "best", is based on a series of comparative measurements. A "ghost excavation" directly aims at the recovery of particular biographical traces of particular individuals.

The borrowing of tech devices from other disciplines and methodologies means there is an acceptance of these devices in the analysis of a haunted space. By doing this, one demonstrates (and reinforces) the use of certain bodies of ideas, techniques, relationships, and understandings regarding process, mediation, and interpretation. An EMF meter measures EMF, not the "cultural gesture" of an emerging presence!

The "ghost hunting" process is physically-based: a measured and recorded space. Shouldn't it be cultural? We are, after all (at least in some cases) investigating human presence, a cultural being, and not a physical "anomaly". If some "ghosts" (if not more) were once human, our focus in the field must center on past cultural behaviors and performance-based "cultural gestures".

Most "ghost hunts" are **"ethnographic displacements" (Alexander 2006).** The "hunt", in the context of this "ethnographic displacement", is one that is **"more engaged in the analysis of space....than in actually experiencing social space as a sincere cultural participant" (2006:53).** Is it any wonder that many "hunts" record EVP's with "Get Out!" being recorded?

In order to re-cover these "cultural gestures" in the field, we must re-think "who" we may be encountering at these haunted sites. And we must be aware of "who" our primary <u>subject</u> of study may be. In the process, we can move from a "hunt" to an "excavation"!

On the "Scent" of a "Cultural Gesture"

Something smells at haunted locations! This is not any archaeological bias on my part, from one who has excavated the "rubbish" of past material presence for many years at archaeological sites! The "ruin" of a haunted landscape (its "hauntscape") is <u>also</u> a "smellscape".

Archaeologist Christopher Tilly, in *Metaphor and Material Culture* (1999) recognized that landscapes have the potential to go beyond a visual perspective. This is a vision of **"scape"**, a documentation of remains within the same space, but using other sensory modalities (such as the "smellscape").

The "excavation" of a "smellscape" is no "odorphobia"! It becomes real, not only residual. What is required, however, is a "toposmia", the study of the spatial location of odors, and their relation to particular perceptions of haunted spaces (see also Drobnick 2002). This must be "excavated" at (as) a particular horizon of meaning.

A haunted space is definitely not a "blandscape", an area so empty of sensory elements that it totally escapes our senses to detect something! Though olfactory experiences are inherently discontinuous, fragmented, and episodic, they do exist.

But the scent must be sensed and recorded in context. It must be relative to what occurred in that space in the past. Smell is haunting phenomena. Time plays no role in its manifestation. The memory of a particular scent does not become a past (and forgotten) presence. It can (and does) frequently re-occur.

Smell, on a historic and former bloody battlefield is more than just a moment in history. It can, as claimed by Gaston Bachelard, **"in and of themselves make myths possible" (quoted in LeGuerer 1992:128).** The odor of tobacco and sulphur are prominent smells on American Civil War battlefields. But what of the scent of blood, putrefied remains, body odors, and other smells on these battlefields? They are more absent than present. Why is this?

Smell is a sense that eventually escapes "death". But smell remains incomplete (and inconclusive) without a context to "unearth" it. The context defines when a particular smell has an intrinsic value:

"But when from a long-distant past nothing subsides, after the people are dead, after the things are broken still….the smell and taste of things remain poised a long time, like souls, ready to remind us, waiting and hoping for their moment, amid the ruins of all the rest" (Proust 1970:36).

The sense of smell comes into play at moments of materialization (presence) and de-materialization (absence), when someone is coming into being and when they are "passing away". Why then is there so little olfactory "After Death Communication" (ADC) on American Civil War battlefields?

Are there "signature scents", perhaps an "Alabama scent" or a New York scent" on these battlefields? What about the sense of scent of former centers of mass epidemics (such as Philadelphia in 1793; New York in 1849; New Orleans in 1853) Are there horizons of meaning, relative to these particular scents? I excavated, and lived near, the medieval "Black Death" pit in Winchester, UK (next to Winchester Cathedral in 1969). Yet I did not awaken at night to some "anomalous" smell.

What about those "sacrificial altars" at Aztec sites in Mexico? I have worked at some, and visited others. There are no "ghostly" presences, or smells of decaying flesh. What about the "priest holes" in the UK, those enclosed spaces of concentrated fear and emotion? Are they "smelly" today?

I spent six months on an archaeological survey in the eastern part of South Dakota, along the James River, in the 1970's. I saw, entered, and experienced numerous abandoned buildings and remote former sites of habitation. I did not sense nor smell anything "different" in these structures.

The list goes on and on. There are so many unanswered questions about olfaction at sites of potential haunting certainties. Still, I believe that we should be extremely careful with smells, and take any haunting experience with a "grain of salt", so as not to give the experience a more "flavorful" interpretation.

Smelling an odor, however, that is clearly out of context with the contemporary surroundings is essential to olfactory ADC. This is one "cultural gesture" in a particular horizon of meaning that we will continue to excavate in order to "gasp" a distinctive odor at these haunted locations.

Haunted Aural Awareness

Do we "hear" past presence in a haunted location? Does auditory memory play a large role in "hearing" a haunting? Are we "listening" correctly? In a "ghost excavation", the cognizance of aural sensory awareness is critical for some "hauntscapes" especially, I propose, on American Civil War battlefields.

An understanding of sound, and its meaning, is important for ghost research because:

"sounds and their original context are stored in memory as patterns….and the sound, if heard again, usually brings the entire complex back to life" (Truax 1984:50).

By using cultural situational scenarios and "soundmarks" (recognizable sounds for a particular group of people or individuals in a particular time and space) during a "ghost excavation, we can establish context for any manifestations that immediately occur during the investigative performance. It is also significant that:

"a particular pattern of sound always produces the same response" (Ibid: 50).

This indicates the importance of sound resonance <u>and</u>, repeating the investigative practice at a later date, the occurrence of a reiterative (repeatable) manifestation, further documenting a contextual link between past recognition and a contemporary performance practice.

Anomalous auditory phenomenons are often reported on a battlefield during "ghost hunts", as well as by casual visitors. The auditory "anomaly" is the most frequent type of manifestation that occurs on American Civil War battlefields (Nesbitt 2005:16). However, without a thorough understanding of aural sensory awareness, understanding the importance and presence of past "acoustic shadow", and a thorough soundscape analysis, those frequent reports of perceived rifle and cannon fire, the sounds of "marching troops", and other "sounds of battle" become highly suspect.

Auditory sensory awareness has three components:

1. **Detection:** This is the sensation of a sound;
2. **Perception:** This is the recognition of that sound; and
3. **Affect:** This is the meaning of that sound.

The awareness of a sound requires <u>active</u> participation. This is focused "listening", a directed concentration. This is what occurs during each scenario we enact in a "ghost excavation".

The detection of sound cannot be a secondary sensory awareness, a "side-bar" to other sensory phenomenon that is occurring elsewhere, or a focused gaze on what is occurring with the electronic devices. If awareness is divided between various simultaneous perceptions, it can lead to a false or inaccurate "recognition" of auditory phenomenon.

If we "hear" a distant sound, but were focused on something else at the same time, we were not "listening". Hence, our perception and the "affect" of the sound cannot be accurately labeled as something distinct, and certainly not something distinctly different from the surrounding (contemporary) soundscape. Likewise, a non-contextual EVP session, done in a general inquiry sweep ("Is anyone here?"), and detected afterwards (perhaps days later) would <u>not</u> have perceptive or affective significance.

There are major differences between a landscape and a soundscape, the aural component of the landscape. A landscape may be comparatively static (if un-developed), and can appear and sound (at times) to be "lifeless". This is true of American Civil War battlefields that have little tourist or "ghost hunting" movements on it.

Still, these environments, as past soundscapes, may have a rich acoustical presence that may become fused with "presences" to "untrained ears". The perception of a landscape is <u>allocentric.</u> It is relative to a fixed external frame, a visual physicality.

In contrast, a soundscape is dynamic. Auditory events that occur (occurred) there, during a particular past production of space in a particular horizon of meaning is inconsistent. This is because human and non-human (animal) activities fluctuate. The physical aural conditions, at any particular time, can change according to the climatological conditions and other natural/man-made factors.

Another major difference, a significant one, is that a soundscape does not have sensory boundaries. The auditory phenomena in the soundscape are experiential. They are largely defined by the social and natural contexts of interaction. They require animated human/animal activity (or conditions) to produce an auditory event.

The perception of a soundscape is egocentric, and is relative to the sensor. There cannot be a fixed external framework (perceived "haunted" battlefield = "anomalous" sound = "gunfire/artillery") in place. This rigid, "in the box", mentality will skew any perception of a detected sound, and the subsequent "affect" of the sounds heard and recorded.

That is why, in a "ghost excavation", we always conduct a preliminary soundscape analysis at a location. This preliminary "soundwalk" serves as a baseline for subsequent sounds recorded during the performing of the contextual scenarios. In this way, we have more control over the auditory sensual awareness of the particular soundscape that may be manifesting in a particular horizon of meaning (of past production) in the "hauntscape" of a site.

Haunted Spatial Awareness

Contemporary experience in and documentation of (through historical research and published works) a historical space is not the same as a past experience of that same space by the participants in, and occupants of, that space in the past. Leone and Potter, in their book, *The Recovery of Meaning: Historical Archaeology in the Eastern United States* (1988), have effectively argued that those who produced the documentary record were, for the most part, not the same individuals who created the archaeological record (1988:14).

In ghost research, and in our work in the field, we must not confuse what historians and contemporary historical researchers say and "what" and "who" may remain at these historical sites from the past. There is a fine balance between historical documentation, research, perception, and fieldwork at perceived "haunted" locations.

There is <u>also</u> the historic ethnographic record: what has been recorded and documented by ethnographers of past cultural ways and expressions ("gestures"). In a "ghost excavation", we are conscious of these contemporary influences from both the past and the present in our analysis of haunted space.

There are various processes of awareness that come into play in these haunted fields. There is "detection" (in one form or another). This has become a relatively common experience today in ghost research, and occurs through various mediated venues of transmission (TV, social networks, You-Tube videos, paranormal radio shows, and web sites to name a few). This mediation is strongly influenced by individual (or team) personality and/or popularity. It is usually not based on solid ethnographic research.

Then, there is the problem of perception. This is predominately a property of cultural exposure to what is considered "normal" in a given society, but is also influenced by one's own personal experiences (or lack of). What the "label" becomes when we experience something "different" may be a "haunting" or a "normal" part of our environmental and cultural awareness.

An important question is this: are these personal experiences, which help to dictate our perceptions, effective "ghosting" mechanisms that can be used to resonate with past experience?

The concept of "haunting spatial awareness (HSA), used during a "ghost excavation" may be useful in determining this resonance. HSA is an emotional, empathetic, sensory-laden, and behavioral-transforming experience of space. It centers on defining what is "haunted space" or a "hauntscape". A "hauntscape", I propose, has three components:

1. **Haunt Horizon:** This is the distance (in space and time) between the past and the contemporary in terms of cultural behaviors and meaning. A particular site may contain multiple haunting horizons of meaning. In each case, one must decide where to "excavate" (what specific horizon of meaning). This becomes a question of

vertical positioning, not a contemporary horizontal one;

2. **Haunt Arenas:** These are the sensory information memory settings (or SIMS) of different spaces within a particular haunting horizon of meaning. It is here that we "excavate" in a "ghost excavation". These spaces represent particular arenas (or spaces) of particular past acts or habits; and

3. **Haunt Channels:** These are the means of communication that we use to recover "what" or "who" remains from past haunting horizons of meaning. For example, when conducting "ghost excavations" on American Civil War battlefields, we use acoustical resonance, as one means to recover and resonate with those soldiers who man remain.

Together, these three components constitute a "HSA", perceived as a surface assemblage of potential "haunting" certainties of space in a particular "hauntscape".

These haunted spaces are a composite sensory environment of multiple, and sometimes competing, potential haunting horizons, each manifesting their own form of communicative channels. These channels are capable of being sensed, measured, and recorded by a wide variety of individual personalities, each with their own subsets of cultural beliefs. These become personal experiences that are perceived in fragmented or trace forms.

In haunted space, however, there is an unfolding "Darwinian combat", I propose, between a manifestation and its awareness by contemporary individuals. It is only the "strongest" (and most recent) sensory manifestation (occurring between individual perception, instrument efficiency and utilization, and investigative competence) that may be recorded and/or measured (as controlled "remains" from the past). At a haunted site, one must also factor in luck, chance, the un-involved, the dis-interested, the bored, and the skeptic that can (and will) influence perceptions and awareness.

This dynamic percolation of experiences and competency creates "clutter" and competition, leading to further uncertainties. This necessitates a <u>serious</u> investigator to focus on context (when a manifestation occurs) and response (did that manifestation resonate to a particular investigative/participatory act).

How can we bring order and control to this potential "cluttered" and "competing" environmental setting? It is essential that we develop a medium of expression in the areas of potential hauntings that is sufficient and contextual enough to overcome the multitude of contemporary phenomenon (and its potential past counterparts) that occur in particular spaces. This medium of expression, one that we use in a "ghost excavation", is a thorough understanding of the site's haunted horizon, arena, and channels of cultural and social communications.

We must, however, focus our efforts on the arena. The haunt arena is where the investigator is able to connect with past patterns (or fields) of former "occupants" who may still remain. It is in this arena that contemporary physical features, and their functions, become arbitrary (unless they remain unaltered by time). This is a key point because it can affect our awareness of particular horizons of meaning in specific haunted spaces.

For example, in our "ghost excavations" at Burnside Bridge on the Antietam Battlefield near Sharpsburg, Maryland, the bridge (the Union objective), the creek (the obstacle), and the dirt road (the Union attack route toward the bridge) are still there, largely intact (and unaltered) from what occurred there on September 17, 1862. We used that resonating physicality in developing the storyboard for the "excavation".

But what happens when a space, particularly an enclosed space (such as a house structure) has been altered by time and/or cultural preference? If the "ghost" opens his/her "door" in a haunting, the investigator is suddenly now "inside" the sensory "arena" where past memory is taking place. This is not the currently-perceived space, but is rather the "ghost's memory space (the "SIMS").

Similarly, if the "ghost" closes a window from its past, the investigator is "shut out" from that past view and sense of smell of that outdoors (which may be significant). It also alters the potential auditory haunt channels that may be perceived and/or recorded.

When haunt "arenas" are "explored" in silence, such as a "watch and wait" monitoring session (or leaving an audio recorder alone in a space), they produce mostly <u>contextual</u> silence. When the setting becomes a "social space", with resonating participatory acts, it can result in a dramatic increase in manifesting cultural "gestures" (or "signs" of a "cultural" haunting).

Each physical space, in each horizon of meaning, becomes an example (and potential haunting "arena") of the dynamic that social beings create. It shows how they select the use of their physical spaces which, in turn, defines the parameters of the "haunt arena".

No single haunt "arena" manifests all the possible interactions of what occurred there in the past; nor can we perceive all of the manifestations that do occur there. As Henri Bergson, in *Matter and Memory* ((1908)1988) has said:

"There is no perception which is not full of memories....what you have to explain is not how perception arises, but how it is limited...." (1988:33).

In fieldwork, we must **"reduce the potentially infinite we are in contact with….to the cognizably finite…." (Straight 2009).** How do we do this? First, we must understand that perception is limited to what remains in the archaeological record of the past productions of space in each horizon of meaning.

Secondly, what remains is based on the past belief systems of those involved in these past productions of space, as remaining "cultural gestures". The archaeological record must match these remaining "cultural gestures".

Lastly, what remains form a limited part of the panoply of cultural codes that were available in any given society in any particular horizon of meaning in the past. These limited set of codes was further reduced by individuals who chose to remember certain aspects of these limited cultural codes in memory. A "ghost excavation", through a scripted storyboard (both contextual and resonating) is meant to recover at least some of these remaining "cultural gestures", through a thorough and sound knowledge of H.S.A.

The Haunted Nodal Spatial System

To properly "excavate" a haunted site, we need to outline its physical parameters, which is no easy task! These parameters may consist of a surface assemblage of multiple past and contemporary past spaces and behavioral "gestures". In addition, some sites were, in the past, further defined by specific contextual intra-spaces.

Such is the case with many American Civil War battlefields. At these sites, the "K.O.C.O.A.", a military terrain strategy, must be used to resonate with "what" and "who" remains on these battlefields.

In general, a "hauntscape" setting can be perceived as a nodal system that includes a set of potential "subjects" (the investigators and the "ghosts"), together with the potential social relations between them. These relationships, in a "ghost excavation", consist of interaction fields (contextual/resonating cultural scenarios) within specific spaces that recover varying degrees of participation, performances, and emergent manifestations.

The components of this potentially emergent spatial/ nodal memory field consist of four identifiable parameters. These include:

1. **Movements:** This is the flow of emerging manifesting presence, together with their cultural behavioral "gestures" (or "signs") that occur into and out of particular spaces (through a door; down a stairs; up a hill; through a woods, etc.);

2. **Nodes:** These are the particular spaces where activity has been recorded and/or observed. In a "ghost excavation", these spaces are called "S.I.M.S." (Sensory Information Memory Settings);

3. **Hierarchy:** This is the type ("residual or interactive"), variety (sensory elements), and intensity (prolonged/reoccurring) of manifesting "gestures" that are recovered during the performance practices (or "excavation"); and

4. **Surface:** The "hauntscape" is divided into zones (or areas) of documented presence, locations of absence, and areas that have yet to be "excavated" and analyzed.

This nodal "hauntscape" system is "excavated", layer by layer (horizons of meaning), through the immersive technique of performance practices (resonating/contextual cultural scenarios). These scenarios, in order to be effective methodological tools, must contain the following characteristics:

- **Have available a resonating energy source:** This is essential in order to recover and document presence. Fieldwork must be participatory, consisting of specific cultural scenarios in particular spaces within a horizon of meaning (historical/cultural occupation);
- **Have capacity to attain and maintain a resonating state:** This is a state of resonance in which the performance practices and the past cultural activity fields that emerge are met by form synchronization. This means that the manifestations that emerge should reflect what occurred in that space in the past;

- **<u>Be (or become) self-regulated:</u>** Participatory practices, cultural "roles", and their field applications in specific spaces must be controlled and follow strict protocols. An iterative process should be developed and maintained in order to "duplicate" the process at a later date. The process should be based on a particular "ghost script" and outlined "storyboard", that is both historically authentic and culturally-contextual;

- **<u>Maintain presence over periods of time:</u>** Investigations should be performed both in the day and at night, in all seasons, and any day of the week. It is not necessary to restrict the investigation, or become dependent upon, historically-dated events (such as "anniversary" dates). Follow-up investigations are mandatory. The performance practices, as outlined in the "script" must be time and culture "sensitive". They must adhere to particular past social patterns (as a horizon of meaning);

- **<u>Maintain organization/form over time:</u>** The investigative process, protocol, methodology, and "tools" should be maintained, yet evolve as new investigative practices are developed through research and/or new data is recovered in the field; and
- **<u>Behave equifinally:</u>** The use of procedural standardization ("P.O.P.") is critical, even though particular cultural scenarios in specific spaces (and what emerges) may vary. This insures the repeatability of performance practices at a later date, or with changes in the structure of the investigative team.

The Mapping of Haunted Space

How does the external/internal "map" of domestic and landscape space affect its navigation where one remains after death? In this essay, a method to understand these fields of afterlife conscious movement within a haunted site is presented.

A cognitive map of space is **"a private construction that includes a mental response to sensory stimuli modified by personal experience" (Blesser and Salter 2009:46).** This constructed space, I propose, continues after death for some, and is used by "ghosts" to traverse the spaces they occupied in life. Everyone, both "living" and "dead", can only know the space in which their personal experiences were enacted. "Unknown" space, I propose, cannot be part of an individual's mapped "haunted" space.

The mapping of this known, experienced, and constructed space is a:

"process composed of a series of psychological transformations by which an individual acquires, stores, recalls, and decodes information about the relative locations and attributes of the phenomena of everyday life" (Downs and Stea 1973).

In a haunting, a "ghost" becomes attached to a particular place <u>and</u> act(s) performed in that place. It becomes a particular experience of place:

"A place owes its character to the experiences it affords to those who spend time there – to the sights, sounds, and indeed smells that constitute its specific ambience. And these, in turn, depend on the kinds of activities in which its inhabitants engage" (Ingold 2000:192).

Part of the character of a place (perhaps all places) is its "haunting" character. What remains (and manifests) are the experiences of individuals in that space as they <u>produce</u> it and re-produce it. What remains are the "cultural gestures" of that particular production: the sights, sounds, and other sensory elements that were enacted and experienced there. They remain in the form of a "ghost culture" of a particular horizon of meaning.

These past experiences, of what still remains, can be sensed from two perspectives:

- **Allocentric:** This is a perception that is relative to a fixed external frame of reference. This is usually defined as the contemporary (and visible) physical layout; and
- **Egocentric:** This is a perception that is relative to an observer, and what he (or she) sees and senses. This occurs in a contemporary (investigative) and past ("ghostly") sense, the latter possibly including multiple viewpoints from different horizons of meaning.

Each perspective modifies the experience of space. The "excavation" of haunted space should combine the two perspectives, and not separate them:

- A "ghost hunt" uses principally allocentric space – the contemporary physical environment – to record and measure the differences in that space. This assumes a "universal" frame of reference: a kitchen is, and always was, a kitchen; a door is a door; a chair is a chair, etc. ;

- A "ghost" (or "apparition") uses egocentric space, the space that is relative to their cognitive map. This is contextual and culture-specific, and thus differs from one culture to another, and from one time period to another: a "kitchen" was not always a "kitchen";

- A "ghost excavation" is a combination of allocentric/egocentric space. It is enacted in known or recorded "S.I.M.S.", which may remain the same, or change through time and/or different cultural occupations.

We cannot "predict" a "ghostly" manifestation or "apparitional" experience. But we can record and document which participatory act resulted in a manifestation in a particular space. We cannot say that, by repeating this same contextual/resonating act, the same (or any) manifesting behavior will be recorded or perceived.

We cannot predict human cultural behavior, so we cannot predict the appearance of a past ("ghostly") presence. We can record and document, however, those correlations between participatory investigative acts and past cultural manifestations that are isochronous: simultaneous with those performance practices.

The mapping of connections between participatory acts in the field in particular spaces, and interactive cultural manifestations is a first step in the "excavation" of haunted space. This is part of an overall research design that utilizes an archaeological sensibility and ethnographic sensitivity in a methodology that we call a "ghost excavation" at haunted (and "ruined") sites.

Bibliography

Alexander, Bryant K. 2006. *Telling Twisted Tales: Owning Place, Owning Culture in Ethnographic Research* in *Opening Acts: Performance In/As Communication and Cultural Studies*. Judith Hamera (Editor) Thousand Oaks, California: Sage. pp. 49-74.

Baert, Patrick 2005. *Philosophy of the Social Sciences: Towards Pragmatism.* Cambridge: Cambridge University Press.

Barbash, Ilisa and Lucien Taylor 1997. *Cross-Cultural Filmmaking: A Handbook for Making Documentaries and Ethnographic Films and Videos.* Berkeley: University of California Press.

Barth, F. 1987. *Cosmologies in the Making: A Generative Approach to Cultural Variation in Inner New Guinea.* Cambridge: Cambridge University Press.

Bell, Catherine 1997. *Ritual Theory, Ritual Practice.* New York: Oxford University Press.

Benjamin, Walter 1994. *The Correspondence of Walter Benjamin (1910-1940)*. Chicago: University of Chicago Press.

1999. *Selected Writings, Volume 2 (1927-1934)*. Cambridge: Harvard University Press.

Bergson, Henri 1988. *Matter and Memory*. New York: Zone Books.

Blesser, Barry and Linda-Ruth Salter 2009. *Spaces Speak, Are You Listening? : Experiencing Aural Architecture*. Cambridge, MA. : MIT Press.

Breglia, L. 2006. *Monumental Ambivalence: The Politics of Heritage*. Austin: University of Texas Press.

Bryman, Alan 2001. *Ethnography*. Thousand Oaks, California: Sage Publications.

Carter, Howard and A.C. Mace 1977. *The Discovery of the Tomb of Tutankhamen*. Dover Publications.

Christianson, Gale E. 1990. *Fox at the Woods Edge: A Biography of Loren Eiseley*. Bison Books.

Downs, R. and D. Stea 1973. *Image and Environment: Cognitive Mapping.* New York: Harper & Rowe.

Drobnick, J. 2002. *Toposmia: Art, Scent, and Interrogations of Spatiality. Angelaki 7 (1)*:31-46.

Eiseley, Loren 1972. *The Night Country.* New York: Charles Scribners Sons.

1975. *All the Strange Hours: An Excavation of a Life.* Charles Scribners Sons.

Finn, Christine A. 2003. *Poetry and Archaeology* in *Ancient Muses: Archaeology and the Arts.* John H. Jameson Jr., John E. Ehrenhard, and Christine A. Finn (Editors). Tuscaloosa: University of Alabama Press. pp. 1-11.

Geertz, Clifford 1973. *The Interpretation of Cultures.* New York: Basic Books.

Gell, Alfred 1998. *Art and Agency: An Anthropological Theory.* Oxford: Oxford University Press.

Gordon, Avery F. 1997. *Ghostly Matters: Haunting and the Sociological Imagination.* Minneapolis: University of Minnesota Press.

Gramm, Kent 2002. *Somebody's Darling: Essays on the Civil War.* Bloomington: Indiana University Press.

Harrison, Rodney and John Scofield 2010. *After Modernity: Archaeological Approaches to the Contemporary Past.* Oxford: Oxford University Press.

Heuer, Kenneth (Editor) 1987. *The Lost Notebooks of Loren Eiseley.* Boston: Little Brown & Co.

Hodder, Ian 1978. *Social Organization and Human Interaction: The Development of Some Tentative Hypotheses in Terms of Material Culture* in *The Spatial Organization of Culture.* Ian Hodder (Editor). London: Duckworth. pp. 199-270.

Holtorf, Cornelius 2007. *Learning from Las Vegas: Archaeology in the Experience Economy. SAA Archaeological Record Volume 73, May.*

Ingold, Tim 1992. *Editorial* in *Man* Volume 27, No. 4: 693-696. December.

2000. *The Perception of the Environment: Essays on Livelihood, Dwelling, and Skill.* London: Routledge

Latour, Bruno 1993. *We Have Never Been Modern.* Cambridge: Harvard University Press.

Law, John 2004. *After Method: Mess in Social Science Research.* London: Routledge.

Lefebvre, Henri 1991. *The Production of Space.* Oxford: Wiley-Blackwell.

LeGuerer, Annick 1992. *Scent: The Essential and Mysterious Powers of Smell.* Richard Miller (Translation). New York: Kodansha.

Leone, Mark P. and P.B. Potter (Editors) 1988. *The Recovery of Meaning: Historical Archaeology in the Eastern United States.* Washington, D.C.: Smithsonian Institution Press.

Gonzalez-Mendez, M. 1998. *Arquelogia y Desarrollo Local: La Arquelogia del Paisaje como Recurso para el Desarrollo Integral de Areas Rurales. Cadernos de Arquelogia & Patrimonio* 7/8: 53-63.

Meskell, Lynn 2008. *Memory Work and Material Practices* in *Memory Work: Archaeologies of Material Practices.* Edited by Barbara J. Mills and William H. Walker. Santa Fe: School for Advanced Research Press. pp. 233-243.

Nesbitt, Mark 2005. *The Ghost Hunters Field Guide: Gettysburg and Beyond.* Gettysburg: Second Chance Publications.

Nora, P. 1989. *Between Memory and History: Les Lieux de Memoire. Representations* 26: 7-24.

Olivier, Laurent 2001. *The Archaeology of the Contemporary Past* in V. Buchli and G. Lucas (Editors) *Archaeologies of the Contemporary Past.* New York: Routledge. pp. 175-188.

2008. *The Dark Abyss of Time.* Paris: Seuil.

Proust, M. 1970. *Swann's Way.* New York: Vintage.

Richardson, Judith 2003. *Possessions: The History and Uses of Haunting in the Hudson Valley.* Cambridge: Harvard University Press.

Robinson, Tony and Mick Aston 2002. *Archaeology is Rubbish.* London: Channel 4 Books.

Sabol, John G. 2008. *Ghost Culture.* Bloomington, Indiana: AuthorHouse Publishing.

2009. *Battlefield Hauntscape.* Bloomington, Indiana: AuthorHouse Publishing.

2012. *Digging Up Ghosts.* Create Space

2012. *Ghost Culture Too.* Create Space.

2012. *Burnside Bridge.* Create Space.

Seamon, David 2013. *Environment and Architectural Phenomenology.* Volume 24.

Shanks, Michael 1991. *Experiencing the Past: On the Character of Archaeology.* London: Routledge.

2012. *The Archaeological Imagination.* Walnut Creek, California: Left Coast Press.

Sheldrake, Rupert 1981. *Morphic Resonance: The Nature of Formative Causation.* Rochester, Vermont: Park Street Press.

Straight, Belinda 2009. *Sensing Divinity, Death, and the Resurrection: Theorizing Experience Through Miracles.* In *The Sixth Sense Reader.* David Howes (Editor). Oxford: Berg pp. 325-337.

Strathern, Marilyn 1988. *The Gender of the Gift: Problems with Women and Problems with Society in Melanesia.* Berkeley: University of California Press.

Thomas, Julian 1993. *The Politics of Vision and the Archaeology of Landscape* in *Landscape: Politics and Perspectives.* Edited by Barbara Bender. Oxford: Berg. pp. 19-48.

2004. *Archaeology and Modernity.* London: Routledge.

Tilley, Christopher 1993. *Art, Archaeology, Landscape (Neolithic Sweden)* in *Landscape: Politics and Perspectives.* Edited by Barbara Bender. Oxford: Berg. pp. 49-84.

1999. *Metaphor and Material Culture.* Wiley-Blackwell.

2004. *The Materiality of Stone.* Oxford: Berg.

Truax, Barry 1984. *Acoustic Communication.* Norwood, New Jersey: Ablex Publishing Corporation.

Turner, Edith 1992. *Experiencing Ritual: A New Interpretation of African Healing.* Philadelphia: Philadelphia University Press.

1996. *The Hands Feel It: Healing and Spirit Presence Among a North Alaskan People.* DeKalb, Illinois: Northern Illinois University Press.

Walker, William H. 2008. *Practice and Non-Human Social Actors: The Afterlife Histories of Witches and Dogs in the American Southwest* in *Memory Work: Archaeologies of Material Practices.* Edited by Barbara J. Mills and William H. Walker. Santa Fe: School for Advanced Research Press. pp. 137-157.

Watson, Richard A. 1991. *What the New Archaeology Has Accomplished. Current Anthropology* Volume 32, No. 3 (June) pp. 275-291.

Wheeler, Sir Mortimer 1954. *Archaeology from the Earth.* Pelican Books.

Wooffitt, Robin 2010. *Toward a Sociological Parapsychology* in *Anomalous Experiences: Essays from Parapsychology and Psychological Perspectives.* Edited by Matthew D. Smith. Jefferson, North Carolina: McFarland & Company, Inc. pp. 72-91.

Photo 26: The author

*John Sabol deep in thought during a Ghost Excavation at
"The Stage Coach House", Lancaster, Pennsylvania*

Biographical Note

John Sabol is an archaeologist, cultural anthropologist, actor, and author. As an archaeologist, he has unearthed past material remains in excavations and site surveys in England, Mexico, and at various sites in the United States (including Eastern South Dakota, the Tennessee River Valleys, and in Pennsylvania). His anthropological fieldwork includes the studies of "spirits" in the religious beliefs of the afterlife among various cultural groups in Mexico (Mixtec, Zapotec, Lacandon, Nahuatl, and Otomi). His acting career includes "ghosting" performances of various characters and scenarios in more than 35 movies, TV shows, and documentaries. He has appeared in the A&E TV series, Paranormal State as an investigative consultant.

He has written twenty books. These include: ***Ghost Excavator (2007), Ghost Culture (2007), Gettysburg Unearthed (2007), Battlefield Hauntscape (2008), The Anthracite Coal Region: The Archaeology of its Haunting Presence (2008), The Politics of Presence: Haunting Performances on the Gettysburg Battlefield (2008), Bodies of Substance, Fragments of Memories: An Archaeological Sensitivity to Ghostly Presence (2009), Phantom Gettysburg (2009), Digging Deep: An Archaeologist Unearths a Haunted Life (2009), The Re-Hauntings of Gettysburg (2010), Digging Up Ghosts (2011), The Haunted Theatre (2011), Haunting Archaeologies (2012), Beyond the Paranormal:***

Unearthing An Extended "Normal" at Haunted Locations (2013), Burnside Bridge Hauntscape: The Excavation of a Civil War Soundscape (2013), Beyond the Paranormal: Learning From The Past of Haunted Locations (2012), Ghost Culture Too: Expanding The Contemporary Reality of Past Interactive Interactions (2012), The Gettysburg Experience: Contemporary Realities of The Past As A Civil War Battlefield (2013), The Absence Above, The Presence Below: The Re-Envisioning of Centralia, Pennsylvania (2013), The Production of Haunted Space: Its Meaning and Excavation (2013)

His recent speaking engagements include the T.A.G. (Theoretical Archaeology Group) Conference at the University of California, Berkeley, at the Space and Place Conference in Prague, Czech Republic, the TAG Conference at the University in Buffalo, New York, Exploring the Extraordinary Conference in York, England, the C.H.A.T. archaeological conference also in York, and the GHost Conference at the University of London, London, England.

His investigative reports have been published in such diverse venues as Haunted Times Magazine, Tennessee Anthropologist, and the online journal, ParaAnthropology. He has been a frequent guest on numerous radio and internet talk shows, among them, Beyond the Edge Radio, The Paranormal View, Para X Radio, Blog Talk Radio, The Grand Dark Conspiracy, and Rusty O'Nhiall's "Mysterious and Unexplained" on PsiFM (Australia). He was a university professor in Mexico for 11 years, teaching both undergraduate and graduate courses on the anthropology of tourism. He has also been featured on public educational TV for U.S. and foreign markets, and has worked on international educational documentaries (in Spain).

He has a M.A. in Anthropology/Archaeology (University of Tennessee), and a B.A. in Sociology/Anthropology (Bloomsburg University). He has also attended Penn State University, the University of Pittsburgh, the University of the Americas (Cholula, Puebla, Mexico), and has studied theatre and method acting in Mexico City.

He can be reached via email at cuicospirit@hotmail.com. His website is: **www.ghostexcavation.com** and he can be found on Facebook ("Ghost Excavations with John Sabol").

C.A.S.P.E.R. logo™© created by Bridget G. Garofalo, reprinted by permission.

Ghost Excavation Books, Inc.,™© logo created by Mel Sabol and Mary Becker, reprinted by permission.

www.ingramcontent.com/pod-product-compliance
Lightning Source LLC
Chambersburg PA
CBHW071038290526
45795CB00004B/1203